THREE CHARACTERS

THREE CHARACTERS
Narcissist, Borderline, Manic Depressive

Christopher Bollas

with

Sacha Bollas, PsyD

PHOENIX
PUBLISHING HOUSE
firing the mind

First published in 2021 by
Phoenix Publishing House Ltd
62 Bucknell Road
Bicester
Oxfordshire OX26 2DS

British Library Cataloguing in Publication Data

A C.I.P. for this book is available from the British Library

ISBN-13: 978-1-912691-81-4

Typeset by Medlar Publishing Solutions Pvt Ltd, India

www.firingthemind.com

Contents

Acknowledgements

I thank Sacha Bollas for the time and thought put into reading the manuscript and then for the questions that he thought derived from some of the participants in the seminars as well as his own interests.

I thank Sarah Nettleton for insisting over the years that these short lectures should be published and for her help in editing them. We have not changed the content of the lectures but have rescued the prose from occasional collapse.

Finally, I thank the participants who took part in these seminars, in Chicago and Sweden. My gratitude to Ulla Bejerholm (Malmo) for her support over several decades. And to William Cornell (Pittsburgh) for inviting me to give the lectures in Pittsburgh in the early part of this century.

About the authors

Christopher Bollas is a psychoanalyst and Fellow of the British Psycho-analytical Society and the Los Angeles Institute and Society for Psycho-analytic Studies.

Sacha Bollas, PsyD, is a psychologist and advanced candidate at the Los Angeles Institute and Society for Psychoanalytical Studies.

Introduction

These essays are based on lectures presented to psychoanalysts, ana-lytical psychologists and psychotherapists who attended the Chicago Workshops (1991–2007) and the Arild Conference (1983–2010). At the Chicago Workshops, groups of eight people would meet three times a year and most members attended for at least ten years. The Arild Con-ference met annually for three days and was attended by thirty clinicians from Sweden and Denmark. Of these, at least twenty-five members attended for about twenty-seven years.

Both groups focused on clinical work. Each meeting would concen-trate on a single case presentation, allowing the presenting analyst to take several hours to present material and to discuss their case in depth. It was common for a case to be re-presented after several years; indeed, in some situations a case was followed over a ten year period.

The participants were senior clinicians. They were well read and were familiar with the seminal psychoanalytic works on character disorders. Many in Chicago had studied with Peter Giovacchini, whom I came to know in the middle 1980s. He also attended the Arild Conference in the 1990s, and so both groups were able to benefit from an understanding of his profound insights into the nuts and bolts of working with the most challenging of character patterns. All the participants knew the standard texts of Otto Kernberg, Heinz Kohut and Harold Searles, and we also studied the writings of André Green, Masud Khan, and other European analysts who had written extensively about character issues.

The essays presented here assume familiarity with this literature or the works of other analysts who have written on the topics. They address selected elements of the three character types, and are by no means intended as comprehensive accounts of all aspects. The particular aim of the lectures the essays are based on was to help clinicians get into the minds of these three personalities, and, keeping with this theme, each chapter ends with a first person narrative of this self's position in the world. Only when we place ourself within the logic of these characters can we begin to identify and empathise with the strategies they have developed to help them survive challenging times.

This exercise of expressing thought in the first person is a technique that I came by at graduate school when I was studying English literature. Confronted with the complexities of seemingly confounding characters, I found that I could approach them more easily if I simply spoke (or wrote) as if I were them. As I followed the sequence of the character as it acted in the world, this would inevitably disclose the logic of the person's character. To take as an example the opening of Melville's *Moby Dick*: we begin with Ishmael, who says, in effect, "I am taking to sea because if I do not I will kill someone." If we follow all his subsequent thoughts and actions, in time their moves repeat axioms that disclose crucial assumptions that guide his personality.

At the outset, it is important to point out that no two borderlines, no two narcissists, and no two manic depressives are the same. Indeed, apart from certain crucial personality axioms, they may have little in common. They will be who they are for many different reasons, but it is nonetheless possible to describe a typical relation between their subjectivity and the world they inhabit. So when we use the descriptions "narcissist", "borderline" or "manic depressive", we are identifying axioms that these individuals share. Each character disorder forecloses the receptive and disseminative fecundity of personality in a different way. In their rivers of consciousness, which will be highly varied, there are types of dam that they will have in common, characteristic mechanisms that operate independently of the quotidien and that are somewhat predictable.

At the root of all character disorders there is mental pain, and the advantage of any character structure is that its repetition makes the person's distress findable. It may take many months of analysis to understand a patient's axiomatic structure, but if we are dealing with a narcissist, a borderline, or a manic depressive, we gradually come to identify and recognise these characteristic traits and the intelligence of their features. Whether we see the problem as mainly biological, or to do with disturbances in the maternal order, or with impossible dilemmas from the real, each disorder is an intelligent attempt to solve an existential problem.

Even though these solutions may in themselves be highly disturbing, if the clinician can grasp their specific intelligence and help the analysand to understand this, then a natural process of detoxification can begin.

CHAPTER 1

The Narcissist

The myth of Narcissus, whose self preoccupation marginalises his relation to the other, may be the first clear character diagnosis to emerge in Western culture.

The story distills a complex refractory meaning in the image of a self-struck Narcissus that is more than surface reflection. It tells us that the nymph Echo has previously been punished by Hera for talking too much. She can no longer start a discussion but can only repeat back what is said by the other. When she sees Narcissus—an adolescent—she is struck by his beauty. She follows him but cannot speak to him. When he sees her he rejects her and she dies, slowly and alone. Later, Nemesis (the goddess of revenge) turns the tables on him. Narcissus comes to a pond that has never been troubled by animals or humans, and as he bends down to drink he sees his own reflection and falls in love with this image. But each time he reaches into the water to embrace himself it shatters. He cannot leave, yet he cannot have the being he desires. Like Echo, he dies from unrequited love.

Putting this together psychoanalytically, the link between the two protagonists might be imagined as follows. An older woman finds a young man. She loves him but he loathes her. In the logic of the narrative,

Narcissus' story then follows hers. But Freud's theory of the logic of sequence suggests that in fact she is rejected by him for the same reasons that she is rejected by others. Even if he is repulsed for physical reasons, as the myth suggests, we know that she has already been rejected for being intrusively talkative.

Psychoanalysis followed the logic of his myth in the analysis of the structure of the narcissistic personality. Modell[1] and others have argued that the narcissist has rejected the primary object, the mother, because she is experienced as too intrusive. In place of the other the self establishes its own image as a new primary object.[2] All is well while the narcissist merely gazes at his image, but any attempt to make contact with it destroys it. Put another way, if the other attempts to engage the self, the self refuses the other and the other fragments. Abjection. Echo tries to engage Narcissus and is rejected. Narcissus tries to engage himself and is destroyed. Both die in their respective attempts to engage an other.

The psychoanalyst working with the narcissist will be familiar with this dilemma. The patient brings troubled waters; he appropriates the lake-session. As the analyst listens, she often struggles to figure out what she can say as the analysand takes up the entire time talking about "narcissistic wounds". These wounds are fragmentations in what should otherwise be an ideal mirror, and the analysand is deeply occupied in the effort to restore this healing pond. The analyst, on the other hand, notes her position as Echo, who can speak only if she reflects the narcissist's wording and interests.

If the Echo-analyst misspeaks then she is suddenly faced with a particular object relation: the lake that fragments the self. Best to remain passive and supportive. Any intervention that differs from the analysand is hazardous.

---

[1] Modell is to my knowledge the first analyst who made this link, which I discovered in his seminar in 1972 in the Department of Psychiatry, Beth Israel Hospital, Boston.

[2] A "primary object" is the infant's and toddler's first experience of "the world". We think of this object as the maternal other. This might seem to place too much of a burden on a mother's shoulders, and it is perhaps more accurate to see that the mother—rather like a newspaper—simply conveys the news. The stories come from many sources.

The self-image

Perhaps the most significant feature of the narcissist is the demand for admiration. However, this can operate at a very subtle level. Although he implicitly idealises himself, he may project this wish-fulfilling fantasy onto other people or onto activities in his life via idealisation. This offers a quid pro quo. You idealise me; I idealise you. He agrees to introduce others into a tacitly idealising society of his own creation. This is the "narcissistic contract": I promote you as exalted; you do the same for me; we offer this service to others. It provides a reassuring base to an otherwise fragile sense of self worth. To live in a world of idealisation is to bask in the radiant light of the idealised object.

The less disturbed narcissist may allow this other to become an intimate—a spouse, for example—and in the best of circumstances this can result in what amounts to a mutual idealising partnership. Indeed, if the partner is also a narcissist then such couples can form a strong bond that, with luck, can weather many a storm.

Let us think about one of the narcissist's assumptions, that the visual takes precedence over the verbal or the symbolic: "I am who or what I appear to be." As we shall see later, this is an important distinction. The narcissist uses language as a sign system. Words are like facial gestures or body positions: they are intended to indicate the pleasure or unpleasure of the narcissist. Although the self's unconscious will always make links at the level of the symbolic order, the narcissist is curiously at odds with his own production of meaning. In the symbolic order meaning can be heard by the other. Indeed, it is shared and can be interpreted. This assumes the notion of mutuality, but the narcissist intends this only as long as his words are accepted as signs of homeostasis-building. The aim is to establish a world of ideals, not ideas. The ideal self or object is an accomplished Gestalt; it inherits the power of the image.

As Lacan emphasises, to speak is to disturb the hegemony of the image; words break up the picture, which is always "worth a thousand words". There is a hatred of the signifier as it decentres the self. It always points elsewhere, and it allows the listening other to become an independent participant in the relational field.

Indeed, some narcissists hate language because it separates them from the hegemony of the image and from their use of the non-verbal to control the other. Typically, whether in a relationship or in an analysis, the narcissist uses facial signs (raised eyebrows, wincing, glancing glumly at the floor), or non-verbal acoustic communications (sighing or coughing), or silence, to assert the self's pre-verbal intentionality. Even when speaking, sometimes quite eloquently, the sum effect of speech is aimed at demonstrating the power the self-as-image has over the other. This is a common characteristic of the charismatic personality. And ironically, even though what is being said may be informative or interesting, the narcissist shows no interest in the content of what is said but only in the fact of saying it. To speak is to defeat speech.

By asserting the priority of the non-verbal world over speech, the narcissist uses a kind of performance art as a medium for manipulating the other and, when it comes to analysis, for defeating the analyst's attempt to create meaning. Instead the narcissist listens to the sound of the analyst's voice, or watches her demeanour. For him, it is in silences that the true analyst resides; in the realm of the pre-verbal.

Ideals and idealisation

During the latency era, most of us form an ideal self. This is not the same as the superego, which is an internal judging agency. The ideal self is an object that the self aspires to be. As we know, adolescence is a crucial era both for self idealisation and for its opposite—a catastrophic dread that the self is an outsider. This is far off indeed from the ideal self. All of us also idealise objects. We create flawless objects that can be the focus of unconditional love, and this accords with the pleasure principle.

The narcissist, however, idealises objects in order to live in a world that, in the most subtle of ways, is without humanity. Human beings are flawed, and this is unacceptable to the narcissist because it leaves him at the mercy of the potential disposition of the other. The idealised self is meant to replace the other, and this is often achieved by proxy, through others who idealise the self of the narcissist. Because he idealises objects, he must narrow the field of those objects in his world that are available for such an investment in order to control them.

The "abject", Kristeva's term for all phenomena marginalised by the personal, social, or cultural demand for a seamless reality, is anathema to the narcissist. Nor can he contemplate Camus' idea that, because we cannot embrace through our rational processes of thought the unthinkable complexity of lived experience, this renders the condition of human being absurd. Both Camus and Kristeva have as a foil the narcissistic structure that refuses to think further about anything outside the grasp of expedient consciousness. When the Nazis exterminated the Jews, they were attempting to rid the world of unwanted parts of themselves by projection. They intended to create a pure race, devoid of any anti-narcissistic dimension; in other words, to eliminate anything that would conflict with the self.

The negative

The narcissist splits the self and his objects into those that are idealised and those that are not. Non-idealised objects are of little interest. They are the abject. But just as idealisation allows for a kind of love life, it also gains energy from hate. The narcissist must find hate objects that are the twins of those that he idealises. We can think of these as *denigrated objects*. The denigrated object is the dustbin that contains the waste matter of human elements that are not part of the narcissist's world. This way, he maintains a link with the discarded through hate.

This brings us to a diagnostic distinction. Some narcissists are sunny people who are fine until they feel their idealised objects to be under threat. Others are preoccupied with the negative, storing away their idealised self and objects in deeply private places. The *positive narcissist* is less disturbed; the *negative narcissist* is the personality that moves this character disorder into the realm of psychosis.

In the negative form we see the foundations of racism, sexism, and genocide. The black, the Jew, the Muslim, the homosexual are denigrated because they become figures for the deposition of the unwanted parts of the narcissistic self. Already hated for their difference, they also constitute the other: the non self. They must be found again and again in order to transform difference into a necessity. They exist in order to assure the self of its own purity.

The positive narcissist

The positive narcissist carefully constructs a world available for harmonious functioning. He is concerned to live in a safe world, untroubled by stimuli that will threaten his sense of good. He does not want deep relations with others as this always involves coming across the negative, so he cultivates what we might think of as convivial acquaintanceships rather than intimate friendships. Unlike the negative narcissist, the positive narcissist may embrace otherness. This may be a successful strategy for a lifetime and friends may never see that such apparent inclusiveness is false; that the aim of such generosity is to fulfill the image he has of the self.

Deep friendship involves a form of reciprocity that the positive narcissist cannot fulfill, but having an acquaintance whom he sees intermittently is fine. Indeed, the less he is known, the more available he is for idealisation. He knows only too well the phrase "familiarity breeds contempt" and he has taken it to heart.

So the positive narcissist has shallow object relations that preserve the self in a kind of American TV commercial aspic. He lives in a voice-over world, saturated by the feel-good. He avoids difference with the other by hanging out with non-controversial objects. He is, for example, a great sports fan. He can love his team, but when it does poorly he can hate it, he can even get angry with individual players but this is safe as he will never come into contact with them. He may genuinely differ with all kinds of decisions and opinions, but this is safe difference. It is not like differing with the other in face-to-face conversation.

Difference is alarming, but it is not catastrophic as long as the self remains in contact with the ideal self-object. However when the other challenges the narcissist by objecting to his position, or indeed his character, he is disturbed. As we shall discuss, the borderline seeks turbulent difference with the object, because emotional turbulence *is* the love object, but this is not so for the narcissist. The defensive ways in which the narcissist copes with difference are too numerous to describe, but the most common protection is the institution of a false self that allows him to handle the other's divergencies of opinion with apparent grace. Like Teflon, it allows difference to slide off him. Indeed, the narcissist may appear strangely un-insultable, and may therefore seem, ironically, to be particularly robust at dealing with difference. But this is because he is not really present. In his place is a substitute self, a false self that allows the true self to hide away in a sequestered space, protected from disturbing events.

In his transference to the analyst he aims to present the self in a good light in order to elicit positive mirroring. If the analyst examines those tactics aimed at eliminating difference, the positive narcissist may readily accept interpretations for proactive purposes: "Yes, you're right, I get that." However, if she says something like: "I think you have agreed so readily because that rather dismisses the topic, doesn't it?", she is likely to be faced with a seemingly bewildered patient.

In the countertransference, she often finds this person initially very appealing; indeed, it is not uncommon for many months, even years, to pass with the analyst content to perform a supportive function for the patient. The narcissist will bring problem after problem from the outside world, and as long as the analyst supports the self's battle with the bewildering and disappointing dimensions of the object world then the analytical couple are fine. But if she seeks to effect character change, through interpretation of the analysand's personality structure within the transference, then she will find that the ready agreements eliminate the cumulative linkage that is the matrix of understanding.

Although the patient may recall prior interpretations, these are kept in isolation and do not lead to the sort of emotional experience that is the engine of personality change. The analyst can then feel that she is regarded as something of a troublemaker, accused of being unnecessarily disruptive to the patient: "Hey, look, I am trying, I really am. I listen to everything you say. I really do get it, I promise you. I think I'm making progress—I'm just a little bit behind." Such comments become familiar, and they eventually reveal themselves as highly effective deterrents to psychic change. The analyst starts to feel as if nothing sticks with this patient and this poses real problems.

Narcissistic licence

All character disturbances operate using differing forms of psychic licence. As I have discussed elsewhere, the hysteric seeks a licence to remain a child so that he can park in the disabled areas of life with a small sign on his lapel that says: "You can't expect me to behave like a grown-up." The borderline has a licence marked "Disabled: out of control." Each licence functions as a kind of permission slip that authorises breakdown of one kind or another. It has many functions, but one of them is that it helps the self explain to the other what happened. "I am sorry I lost it, but I am just too overworked and when that happens I can be overly sensitive."

Narcissistic licence is based upon the inclination to agree readily with the other. He licences the other to disagree with the self. This manoeuvre may lead others to admire him for his ability to stand the wear and tear of the politics of relating. In secret, it is as if he is saying "there isn't anything I can't take".

However, in order to be effective each kind of licence must be accountable to the superego for its internal administration. If the licencee has exceeded the terms of the licence, then there must be a form of punishment. In the case of the negative narcissist, as long as the licence is operating he can often function in highly stressful environments without crashing. But if the licence has not been renewed then, to the amazement of others, he may produce a sudden outburst of rage or break down into a clinical depression. If he blows his right to affiliation with his ego ideal, this can lead to a catastrophic loss of belief in the self. If he has done something that he knows will preclude the repair of the idealised self, he may resort to killing himself in order to avoid witnessing the desecration of the former idealisation. In the most extreme cases, he may even commit homicide.

Narcissistic confession

There is anorther possible strategy: *narcissistic confession*. Most people entering 12-step programmes, such as AA, will "confess" in order to get the truth out and then begin the process of recovery. The narcissist, however, confesses in order to trump his critics. For a period of time he may take out a "confession licence" that enables him to become his own harshest critic. He may appear to be communicating with others. He may appear to be seeking to help them. In fact, he is involved only in the restoration of his self idealisation. This is clinically detectable: the negative narcissist does not really want to discuss his crime. He can lecture on it, but he does not want it investigated in conversation with the analyst. There is a rigidity present that the analyst will sense in the countertransference as a no-go area.

As the narcissist does not want to be in a communicative relation in which the bad and the good will inevitably be mixed together, he also does not want to get inside the other. He is notorious for a lack of true empathy. He will often be capable of a kind of Hallmark Card concern, but in fact this is aimed at warding off deeper involvement with the object.

This strategy enables him to accumulate "frequent card miles" that will lead to the upgrades sought by the narcissistic personality as part of his private, silent journey. It is not surprising that so many narcissists are drawn to Protestant Christianity because then their good deeds are seen and appreciated by God. God is, of course, the quintessential narcissistic love object and good deeds lead to a quality of upgrade that only He can give. This private relation to God, so much more important than relation to mere mortals, is the perfect environment for the narcissist. Indeed, with God as the internal object providing nourishment, He acts as an agent who pushes the narcissist to go out into the world and take part in it. He does not really want to, and he and God know this. But each time he overcomes his wish to remain in sequestration he earns futher upgrade miles. Those who are the recipients of such attention may easily mistake this for the narcissist's genuine investment in others, but it is not. It is a missionary moment and the narcissist will retreat back to his enclave as soon as he can. Church is just about the best place for these sort of contacts, as church is time limited and mediated by other than human dimensions. Indeed, it is a place where out of respect for God people can easily avoid engaging in too many human dimensions. It is not good to gossip in church, or to seduce someone, or to challenge others for their politics. It is simply a place to see and be seen.

We may see how, for the Christian, hell is the ultimate dustbin, the place where all the hated objects go so that Heaven can be a place of pure, uncontaminated ideas. The Protestants solved the conundrum of "we all have bad thoughts, so aren't we all going to hell?" by deciding that it was God's grace that elected those who were to enter Heaven. It was nothing to do with good deeds on earth. For the Christian narcissist, however, upgrades provide a quiet assurance that he will get through the pearly gates.

In the transference, then, this patient is adept at trying to convince the analyst that he is making progress. The analyst may be seduced into thinking that expressions of feeling are genuine signs of effort on the part of the analysand to be a participant in the process. But there is a striking absence of cumulative memory—the building of new psychic structures that is the outcome of the development of meaning. The narcissist continually recounts similar encounters with others and repeats the wish that the analyst be a continuously supportive presence, focusing on problems created by external factors and on how well he is doing in dealing with adversity that is not of his making.

Narcissistic declaration

Of course, it may not be long before the partner of a narcissist becomes aware that his apparent generosity and openness are actually a subtle form of non-relating. The narcissist's challenge will usually come as a result of the other's complaint or lament. A typical solution to this is *narcissistic declaration*. "Well that is what you think. This is what I think. So that's the end of the discussion." But when challenged further, the narcissist's underlying aggression may become palpable. If the partner persists in seeking answers to certain questions, she is met with a "leave me alone or else" communication. If narcissistic declaration does not work then the most typical second line of defence is *narcissistic withdrawal* when the narcissist simply walks away.

Typically, he might say to the analyst "Well I appreciate that is your view, but I think the problem is…" thereby undermining the acquisition of knowledge. This can be very unsettling to the analyst, especially if she espouses the patient's right to free association and the value of the dialectics of difference, or if she believes that analysis should be a process that involves the democratic, near-symmetrical relation of the two participants.

This analysand is likely to have learned the rules of analytical culture, sometimes down to the fine print. Confronted with an interpretation aimed at helping him become conscious of an enactment in the session, he may say "Well I don't know what to make of what you have said. But anyhow I have a dream to report. So I'll do that and we'll see where we go." This may be enough to sidetrack the analyst from focusing on character analysis. It is a clever strategy; it employs the very essence of analysis, turned against itself to promote a defence against interpretive contact.

Narcissistic law

The psychoanalytical theory of law-making focuses on the oedipal period. The father is the lawmaker. In Lacan's reading of Freud, the name of the father stands for the rules and regulations of a culture. When the child of four to six years old is engaged in oedipal struggle, he discovers that he can no longer have direct access to the mother. Indeed, he learns that his existence was preceded by that of mother and father together, and in particular by their sexual life. If he is to develop, he is now required to integrate the father into the self system. When the mother says to the naughty child, "I will tell your father when he gets home," she is not simply referring to her husband, she is invoking the Name of the Father, referring the child to the law that he must obey if he is not to be punished.

This type of experience structures the personality so that the self can assimilate reality, relate to it, and go on to use it in creative and productive ways. The narcissistic personality, however, has circumvented this important moment. To understand this, we have to see how and why the narcissist destroys the maternal object that is the precondition for the formation of the self's law.

Narcissistic emptiness

All of us learn that at times we have to fall back on our own self when others let us down. The narcissist, however, has come to an early decision that the primary other cannot be relied upon, and to varying degrees he will find ways to live in psychic isolation, with the self as the most reliable replacement for the other.

The negative narcissist then goes about getting as many others as possible to love the self. A split has occurred in the personality. The true need for intimacy and communication is split off and the self proceeds on the assumption that he must just get on with it alone. But the absence of a history of self–other mutuality has a structural effect. As a small child, the negative narcissist fails to seek objects that will nourish the self and create a continuous linking with the object world. This is a vital exchange that involves a fluid interplay between external reality and our internal world which, in turn, allows our subjective life to make a contribution to the real. The history of such an exchange normally becomes an internal structure whereby the self communicates with objects and empathically identifies with them, thus gaining the richness found in the object world. Unlike the schizoid who, even though she might appear cut off, does introject objects and may develop a very rich internal world, the narcissist's internal world is empty. Little thought is given to internal life and reality is replaced by the virtual.

Narcissistic emptiness is therefore the result, not of actual deprivation, but of a missing internal structure. The absence of a history of engagement with the object world, one that would have populated the mind with paradigmatic assumptions about the richness of difference and exchange, is offset by the construction of an ideal self. Such emptiness means that there can be little internal nourishment, and this sponsors an intensification of greed, in which the self is never going to be satisfied. In the clinical situation, any positive comment the analyst makes to the narcissist is quickly consumed, not in order to be digested as the basis of further thought, but so that it can be ingested immediately so that the hungry mouth can be kept open. The narcissist may appear to be a very good listener, but actually he is operating from Bion's "–K" position. He takes in only beta elements and what appears to be intense listening is based on his greed.

The child who sets out on the narcissistic course of development becomes his own lawmaker; he is a law unto himself. Having replaced the mother with the self, the narcissist lives in a world of his own creation. Of course this cannot actually be true—we are all dependent on others in many ways—but his knowledge of such dependence, indeed of otherness itself, has been negated by him in order to annihilate the maternal order. At the crucial period of the anal phase, every child must exchange the pleasure principle for the reality principle. He must give up the pleasure of unrestrained defecation and urination in order to please the mother who urges him to do this in order to earn her admiration. The anal period introduces the first substantial conflict, as the child is forced to recognise the existence of a social world to which he has to adapt.

Some children resist this and may battle the mother for a long period of time. The narcissistic child, however, may already have constructed a false self that obscures his narcissistic assumptions. Narcissistic law resolves forever the question of adaptation to reality.

Narcissistic withdrawal

Unlike the aloofness of the schizoid personality, the narcissist's withdrawal is an action, aimed at eliciting from the other some form of apology or reparation that will restore narcissistic equilibrium. The narcissist's need for approval and external admiration is too great to sustain a period of withdrawal for long. For the schizoid, the withdrawn location is perfect, as this self much prefers the world of internal object relating to self–other relatedness. The narcissist, however, depends on external sources of supply. This derives from the use of the ideal self, a projected image that can be visible in hallucinatory moments.

The positive narcissist's withdrawal is aggressive: it aims to force the other to make amends. He may try to force reparation from the analyst: "See how you have hurt me by what you have said." With the negative narcissist, however, the act of withdrawal will be more pernicious. He can retreat into a dark silence, refusing to speak for days, weeks, or even months. The analyst tries to contact him, but both the form and the content of such efforts fall on seemingly deaf ears. The aim, here, is to *destroy* both the meaning of what the analyst has said and the form of the delivery. The analyst is invited to feel, not only that nothing she says will get through, but that the very act of speaking is of no use. In short, she begins to experience her own annihilation. If she tries to interpret this to the patient she will be met either with silence or with violent innocence: "I really don't know what you're talking about." We shall return to this later when discussing "bad faith".

The narcissistic contract

The other must be need-satisfying. In turn the other will receive a certain consistent form of provision. The narcissist needs to live in a stable, reliable, and predictable world. He therefore needs his other to be reliable, even if this takes the form of being reliably eccentric, or reliably hysteric.

When the other is reliable in this way then the narcissist can form a *narcissistic bridge* to the other as a structure. This means that he can programme the other's requirements into his own system of being and relating to her. This comes close to an obsessive-compulsive use of structure-as-other, but the narcissist is quietly dehumanising the other by replacing her with a set or matrix of expectable needs that can be met by a reliable set of provisions that do not trouble the narcissist.

So if he knows that his partner likes a particular TV programme, a type of music, a set of friends, all these objects will be programmed into what the narcissist provides. He himself is not at all interested in the qualia of these objects. They are intended only as narcissistic peace offerings used to gain in return those provisions needed by the self. These might be, for example, the need to be left alone to read the newspaper for an hour or so each evening, or the need to spend time every evening in the local gym. Such needs are unlikely to be challenged if there is a *narcissistic contract* between self and other.

In analysis, this person can be an engaging gift-giver, offering interesting titbits of news from the world, or compliments to the analyst for helping him with particular problems. He may bring actual gifts— clippings from a magazine, or a new book. This steady stream of offerings makes the analyst feel churlish if she proceeds to focus on character features, as such discussions will evoke unwelcome feelings in the patient. This is particularly true if she elects to explore how the gift-giving is itself part of an effort to control her with generosity.

Narcissistic guilt

Given all of the above, a question arises. If we assume that the narcissist unconsciously knows that he has destroyed the primary object, will this not produce guilt? The answer is that of course it does. And many of the sociopathic stratagems of the narcissist are aimed at deferring the consequences of guilt. To my way of thinking, deferring is crucial because it is the alternative to acceptance. As long as he thinks that one day—a day that will never come—he will confront his guilt, then there is a pay-off: guilt is assuaged by a promise. The promise is that the self will engage in an outwardly penitential existence, seeking forms of masochistic punishment that will earn "frequent masochism miles" in the upgrade programme.

In order to allay guilt, he may go on *narcissistic pilgrimages*. Friends not seen in years, professional associations neglected for decades, tasks long unfulfilled, suddenly become the object of a full-on intense commitment. The aim is the act itself: the act of suffering as he fulfils contact with lost objects.

Sometimes that lost object will be the analysis. After years of work that often leave the analyst feeling that she is not getting through to him, suddenly he embarks on an intense and moving articulation of what he has learned about himself in the analysis and how he feels he is changing. The analyst can get caught up in this intense engagement, her long marginalised wishes for therapeutic effectiveness now seemingly coming to fulfillment.

How hard it is, then, in the countertransference for the analyst to find that on the following Monday, or in a week's time, the relation is back to where it has always been. Since the patient seems to have no memory of the encouraging progress that has just taken place, the analyst is left to slide back into a limited and somewhat meagre existence.

For the narcissist, this has been a pilgrimage, with the aim of paying off that guilt stored in him for his long-standing refusal to be analysed. However, efforts such as this to mitigate guilt do not work. Murders have been committed, people destroyed, meaning evaded, lives not lived.

What can the narcissist possibly use to remedy this? He will be able to say, unconsciously of course, that he wielded power. "I never asked anyone for anything in my life" is the narcissistic credo. But having failed so many, this is a negative quid pro quo: you failed me/I fail you. Guilt is not negated but it is diminished, reduced to something anodyne: a kind of psychic luxury. Who needs it?

Narcissistic greed

The narcissist must populate his universe with objects that will satisfy his greed. He is the consumer par excellence.

As we shall see when we explore the borderline personality, there is a useful distinction to be drawn in connection with the primary object, following Winnicott's theory of the object-mother and the environment-mother. We have discussed the narcissist's response to the failures of the object-mother, but he finds in the environment-mother (or the world) objects that will mirror the self. Thus, he invests in certain objects in the world around him that support the self's need to be mirrored in a positive way. Such objects can be people (often grandparents) or objects, such as toys, animals, or the body-self.

Later we shall return to this aspect, but for now we shall focus on how narcissistic consumption of such worldly goods fails to solve the narcissist's underlying dilemma. Indeed, as life goes on, the narcissist realises that no matter how much he consumes, he cannot rid himself of the feeling of an internal void.

Narcissistic horror

There are some severely disturbed narcissists whose awareness of their emptiness causes them to experience a sense of horror that is often focused on the realisation that they have not really lived their life.

As we have seen, loss of intimacy with the primary object is implicit in the character structure of the narcissist, but when he registers the fact that he has lost the possibility of living his life as it could have been, this is a source of great mental pain and an acute sense of loss. Hard on the heels of narcissistic horror comes a depression that may never resolve itself, but, as long as it does not lead to suicide, it is at this point that the positive narcissist is most available for psychic change.

Psychoanalysis can offer both a relationship and a historical reconstruction that helps this person feel and see why he has become so isolated, and why he was driven to do what he did. Depression leads to a true helplessness that necessitates reliance on the analyst. By carefully and lucidly linking up character structure to psychic and relational history, the analyst makes it possible for this person to understand himself. In doing so, many of the narcissistic defences ease, at least enough for the patient to begin to make use of the otherness of analysis and the analyst.

The negative narcissist, however, will take a very different turn in the road. Faced with the failure of his demands to be met and caught up in the depression of such failures, he becomes enraged and vengeful. For him, the only way to redress this loss is to destroy as many parts of his life as he can, and this includes people. The analyst and the analysis are in his cross-hairs as a prime target for destruction.

A great deal could be said about this topic alone, and I find the writings of André Green and Herbert Rosenfeld essential in attempting to understand the negative. I have said that the narcissist replaces the primary object with the self and the ideal self. Rosenfeld concentrates on the destructive side of this action, and in the case of the negative narcissist he is right to do so. It is as if the destruction of the object leaves a mnemic trace of the power of this destructive act, and it is in this sense of power that the self finds compensation for what was not there. So for the negative narcissist destruction is an alternative to creative life. Indeed, Rosenfeld believes that the negative narcissist splits off and eliminates the loving and creative sides of the self, whilst the remaining parts behave like a mafia gang led by a mafioso.

The aim of the negative narcissist is now to find in the omnipotence of destructiveness a form of nourishment derived from the malignant breast. Like Iago or Macbeth, in feeding off evil thoughts the negative narcissist finds a breast that is always there and will be unfailingly reliable, and in this tainted way he sets up a perverse relation to a certain kind of other. These people populate hate-based organisations, such as religious fundamentalists or paramilitary groups that enjoy violence and killing. It is not difficult to see why they choose to join such groups; it is imperative to kill off the loving and creative side of the self.

The narcissist does not begin life with this degree of entrenched negativity. As a toddler and as an oedipal and latency child, although he may have killed off the primary object, thereby killing off affections, he will have set up an ideal self. There will have been a period of hope. But the heroes of this child's life will only be sustainable as delusional objects.

At what point does a representation such as the ideal self become a delusion? This is a hard question to answer. When the mental pain arriving out of hopelessness becomes too great, the negative narcissist attaches himself with increased ferocity to the ideal self. That ideal can then mutate from something close to a real-self possibility into a super hero. In the extreme, this might be a Hitler or a serial killer. In most cases, by the end of adolescence the negative narcissist has killed the ideal self. This is now a double murder. The primary object has been killed, but so too, now, has its stand-in.

The negative narcissist appears cynical, sarcastic, and cold. He will go to work, he may marry, he may even have children, but he is emotionally unmoved by his life. His only attachment is to the mafia leader inside his mind that trashes creative existence.

Narcissistic outbursts

These tactics that aim to preserve the narcissistic strategy of displacing the other with the self will not succeed for a number of reasons. One of the most challenging clinical encounters for the analyst is when this person has a sudden and sometimes violent outburst of grief, remorse or death-driven insight. These outbursts come with no warning, and no discernible context that might allow meaning to be derived from them.

It is as if a part of the personality has escaped from the cult organised by the mafia boss; it gets just far enough to cry out to the other before it is shot on the spot and silenced. Although such moments are not uncommon, the analyst working with the narcissist will always be surprised when they occur. She may attempt to refer back to them and to connect with the failed escape, but the narcissist, now fully under the auspices of the negative, will deny its meaning or be indifferent to it.

Why does he seek analysis?

Why would a seriously disturbed person on this narcissistic spectrum choose to have therapy? Thus far I have not mentioned negative hallucination.

Denial of mental and emotional reality is the bedrock of the narcissistic defences, and negative hallucination drives this self's ironic vision of the world. Such a way of seeing operates according to the laws of Bion's –K. The negative narcissist eliminates object possibilities, but in doing so he gradually subtracts from his own mental capacities. After decades of denial and negative hallucination, eventually the non-psychotic parts of the personality have been eroded to such a degree that the self is now functioning as a psychotic character. Denial and negative hallucination are, of course, both on the psychotic side of the defensive spectrum.

The narcissist destroys the primary object and substitutes it with the self. But what kind of self will this be? As Kohut so astutely noted, it is a grandiose self. So we have a grandiose self, now functioning psychotically—eliminating the world rather than taking it in—and gradually the reality of the world becomes shaky. It is not uncommon for the negative narcissist to somatise his situation as a form of defence and for a doctor then to tell him that he suffers from so much stress that he needs therapy. So he may seek this out because of a somatic deterioration, or he may experience a type of depression. And in the severely disturbed negative narcissist, this is likely to be psychotic depression.

The return of the killed

Psychotic depression in the negative narcissist is the return of the killed. The eliminated do not return in representational form, so psychotic depression does not ordinarily move to hallucination. Instead, this depression is a stuporous state in which the self cannot function. It would be easy enough to misdiagnose this person as a schizophrenic, but in the case of the narcissist this depressive breakdown usually occurs late in life, when he may have a relatively normal previous history of hard work, family, and so forth. Typically he simply stops all functioning, takes to his bed, and watches endless TV, talking only in monosyllables.

It may seem curious, given the negative narcissist's capacity for creating an internal situation of mafia power, that suddenly, late in life, he feels that life has no meaning. What has changed? The crucial thing is that he is faced with the reality of Death. This may be triggered by the death of someone in the family, but, more to the point, he suddenly seems to realise that one day he will die. For a killer this is bad news. He has based his way of being on an omnipotence generated by destructiveness, and this is akin to being shoved off the throne. In Rosenfeld's terms, it is the moment when he is kicked out of the mafia.

In short, the negative narcissist has now lost those forms of power that he had previously used to deal with the awful circumstances of his life. For a while, the negative power negated the effect of trauma upon the self. He has experienced a kind of timeless life, a life without guilt or concern, but now death beckons. This loss of power means, of course, the loss of omnipotence. As he has always hated humanity, he cannot be an ordinary human in this midlife crisis. When he has no idea what to do or where to turn, he may criminalise this dilemma. Or he may show up in the analyst's office.

Bad faith

I have deferred until now one of the common characteristics of the narcissistic personality—especially of the negative narcissist—and that is bad faith.

This term was introduced into philosophy by Sartre and then elaborated by Simone de Beauvoir, but I use it in a specific way. A person is in bad faith when he knowingly deceives himself and others. In the analytic situation, this means that speaking in bad faith is consciously aimed at throwing the analyst off track. A patient in bad faith may invent dreams and reports from the day, or he will leave out what he knows to be salient details in order to send the analyst off in the wrong direction. He will note her efforts to understand him but instead of co-operating with that endeavour he will side-step it and defeat it.

The negative narcissist envies the analyst's faith in reason and her personal sincerity. The quietly logical and generative features of the analytical processes are also envied and become objects of hate. By using bad faith the analysand can destroy clinical effectiveness, creating an empty figure and an empty process that become the projective identifications of the narcissist's vacant self.

Experienced analysts can usually discern when this is taking place, but finding the right time to word this to the patient is crucial and vital. In doing so the analyst enters a very dark realm, crossing the River Styx into the psychopathic world of the deadened-that-exist-to-kill. Few other challenges in psychoanalytical work are as arduous as this one. There is no guarantee that addressing this will be efficacious—after all, it is not a matter of making something unconscious conscious—but there is a sense that speaking to this issue represents a court of last resort. How will it be received? How might it bring the analysand back into some contact with the life instincts?

The axioms and logic of the narcissistic personality

What are the psychodynamic and the object relational axioms that constitute the logic of this personality? For the sake of clarity, I shall present these in summary form, as though speaking in the voice of the narcissist.

1. I find the intimate other—the one who aims to know me—invasive, unreliable, and appropriative.
2. I nullify the effect of this other by not seeing them.
3. I too am invisible. As I am not present, I am not responsible for relating.
4. In place of the intimate other I select non-invasive selves who will mirror me as I will mirror them. With detached others, detached relating is successful.
5. If I am a positive narcissist I can get by in life by apparently embracing a multitude of friends who will provide positive mirroring experiences, so there is no need for intimate engagement.
6. I like happenings, parties, and accidental intimacies, so I find ways of sourcing them and taking part.
7. When my limited needs for nurturance go unmet, I can easily dump the person and find ready-to-wear others who will give me what I require.
8. I use the stolen other's breast as a form of sustenance, without knowing how I have gained it.
9. I cannot make this last because it is not self-generated. It was created by an other whom I can hate and envy.
10. When things start to be unsatisfactory, I drop people and move on.
11. I am pursued by a shroud of guilt which persecutes me, but I defer the day of judgement.
12. Eventually I have to experience the ineluctable disappearance of my illusions and face my maker—with myself as murderer. I have lost all I have, and I sink into self-hate which allows me to direct my rage against the final object.
13. A desperate final choice is to hasten my own death or to kill others, so that we all go down together under the spell of the death drive.
14. But if things are less dire—maybe I am part of a comfortable retirement community—then I can look in the mirror and declare undying love for myself.
15. To be with others was always a loan programme. Commitment to them was never a possibility. I can be committed only to my one true love: my self.

Clinical issues

Both the positive narcissist and the negative narcissist present clinical challenges that are by no means easy for the analyst. The following guidelines address some aspects that we can keep in mind.

Kohut was right about the need in the narcissist for an idealising transference. In my view, in order for the narcissist to have an experience of intimacy, a substantial period of time should be allowed for the transference to settle before it is interpreted. As the analysand develops this new relationship and the experience gradually connects him to the primary object, there is decreased need to live through the image of the ideal self. Defences such as denial, negative hallucination, and grandiosity diminish as the analytical relationship offers him a real-life and real-time alternative to delusional life.

Eventually, it will be necessary to help him understand his way of thinking, but timing is everything. Kohut rightly points out that it is important to examine any empathic failures on the analyst's part, but ultimately the real crisis emerges when the patient experiences true disappointment both in the analyst and in the self.

If all goes well, disappointment in the self and the other leads to a *realisation*. In Bion's language, this is based upon a preconception that allows for a concept that neither the self nor the object world is perfect. This permits the self to receive back split-off parts that have been denied, and this brings a capacity for ordinary depression. This progress is contingent upon the prevailing directions of the life instincts, and it presupposes that analyst and analysand find positive vectors in the work that can facilitate these changes.

More often than not, however, a different clinical picture emerges in the transference, one that proves to be deeply challenging to the analyst. Assuming that, over time and with patience, the analyst has carefully brought the narcissist to positions where the underlying axioms of the self are discussable, she may then find herself confronted by a new phenomenon in the work, revealed through a new set of statements that seem disabling.

"I have heard what you have said but I'm not sure I understand it." When she tried to examine exactly what it is that the patient has not understood, using what feels by then like a well-established understanding, he might say "Yes, I know, I'm sorry. It's just that I can't quite grasp the real meaning of what you're saying." He then reports events in his life that seem curiously retrograde, demonstrating an undoing of the insights supposedly gained through the years of analysis. When the analyst points out that he seems to be going back over things that they have been discussing for a long time, he seems bewildered. It is as if he has learned nothing in all these years of work.

He may begin to miss sessions, or arrive late, seeming curiously indifferent to analysis and demonstrating a weariness with it all. Whereas previously he seemed to listen with some regard for what the analyst had to say, now he replaces what she says with his own interpretations, or simply talks on as if nothing had been said. In the countertransference, the analyst feels as if the patient has assumed the role of analyst, thereby removing her from the scene.

In addition, periods of reflection are now usurped by *refractive* speech. Whatever the analyst tries to convey comes back bent out of shape, a part object of what has been said, woven into a "meaning" that moves away from the analyst's communications. The "invariants" of analysis, to which Bion referred, seem no longer to exist.

At the same time the analyst may start hearing that the patient has turned to others in his world who seems to be performing a quasi-analytic function. She may discern specific elements of what she has said to the patient in his accounts of how he is helping others with their problems.

At this point, the analyst's countertransference is particularly important in understanding what is taking place in the transference. She feels as if she has been marginalised or removed, as if something has been stolen from her. There is often a sense that the patient seems aggressively self-satisfied, the fount of a new kind of wisdom that he is disseminating to the community. Attempts to address this phenomenon meet with an increased psychopathic mobility on the analysand's part: missing sessions, arriving late, announcing that he does not think he can take more analysis, and increased aggression towards any effort on the analyst's part to interpret what is taking place. At the same time, she has an uncomfortable sense that her interpretations are bordering on the inquisitorial, that she is being forced into fulfilling not simply ego functions, but superego functions as well. It feels as if this is now at best a game of chase, at worst something negative and horrifying.

What is taking place?

At the point in the psychoanalysis of the negative narcissistic personality when, through patient work, the core conflict is finally being addressed, the narcissist regresses to very early object relating. He returns to the breast in order to steal it, to appropriate it for the self, and he proceeds with a nipple-breast that is allied to the thumb in a nipple-thumb-sucking self nourishment. The emotional relation to the (m)other is destroyed and the presumed source of nourishment—the analyst's mind and discourse—is appropriated.

The patient will not, of course, benefit from this action. Indeed, he is caught up in a profound delusion that has appropriated enough of the analyst's insightful feedings to construct the illusion of a breast from which he can imbibe the self's own production of food-for-thought. Analysis of this feature of a transference is exceedingly difficult, but if patient and analyst can survive it then the core conflict of the narcissistic personality can be profoundly helped. But there are analysands who experience this as the homicidal action of an analyst-murder. If his negative structures are too galvanising and empowering to be given up, the analysis will be destroyed.

So the narcissistic personality constitutes a spectrum from the positive to the negative. The negative narcissist presents profound clinical challenges to the analyst, whose psychic life (and on rare occasion his actual life) becomes the target of narcissistic murder.

CHAPTER 2

The Borderline

The borderline personality can be regarded as the favoured diagnostic inhabitant of the late twentieth century, just as today that privilege has been usurped by the so-called bipolar personality. When we look back on the explosion of the "borderline" diagnosis in the clinical population, we may realise that many of these individuals were in fact hysterics. During this period, psychiatrists and therapists had desexualised their analysands, and in place of thwarted desire they saw a fractured ego.

However, the borderline personality certainly exists and it offers a profound presenting picture.

Mental pain

This is a person in unremitting mental pain. Unlike the hysteric, no secondary gain is achieved through her suffering yet, unlike the narcissist, the borderline does not wish to dismiss it. Indeed, she seems to seek it.

Since the borderline requires an other to whom such pain may be attached, she is often in a long-term relationship that is extremely conflicted and fraught. Every day there is yet more pain. The other, whom she repeatedly accuses of causing this, seems to the analyst after a while to be indistinguishable from the internal object that evokes the pain.

This person seems driven to select from the facts of life those mental objects that will evoke extreme anxiety, profound disorganisation, harrowing depressions, and endless rage. This cocktail, a combination of intense affects and ideas, forms a matrix of mental pain that seems to have a life of its own. Unlike the mental pain of the schizophrenic, which is objectified as something external, unwanted, and avoided at all costs, the borderline amps up the pain into a frenzied embrace that exceeds the economy of desire resident even in the most extreme forms of masochism. It is the shadow of an object that relies on the borderline's determination to appropriate it by taking its pain into the self.

Dream life

For the borderline, dream life is so burdened by the mental anguishes of the day that the dream experience is experienced as nightmarish, even if the content appears benign or banal. The archaic object relation called up by dreaming—the self's foetal and infantile relation to the maternal other—is suffused with anguish. As the processes of condensation bring disparate thoughts together into single images, the matrices of self experience that were undifferentiated during the day continue at night.

This merger of day and night means that dreaming and perceiving blend into one another. The borderline does not have a cognitive problem in distinguishing between dream and reality, or between hallucination and perception of external reality, but it is as if this is of no real emotional matter. Dreaming and living both feel contaminated by violently disturbing stimuli.

Somatisation

The cumulative impact of this endless life in hell is that borderline personalities often somatise this state. Unlike the hysteric, for whom conversion-somatisation symbolises an unconscious idea, borderline somatisation is a corporeal register of a mind that is unable to contain the vexing effects of mental contents. Unlike the narcissist, who somatises in order to localise and bind distress, the borderline's somatic state is not binding but is simply a corporeal extension of mental anguish.

This soma is not simply an extension of the mind, or the body as "thinker"; it expresses mental states as if it were part of a thought-continuum with no boundary between mind and body. When she is talking to the analyst, the borderline may sneeze, cough, itch, and scratch, or move in lurches, as if propelled by thoughts. For the recipient of such communication the body seems to be expressing ideation in a manner that feels disturbing.

In reality, the borderline will often neglect her body. She will present herself as always exhausted, and her constant state of fatigue contributes in turn to mental difficulties. It is not just that she might be too tired to think because it has been a rough week. Most people can point to difficult periods in life that caused fatigue. But with the borderline there will be no single event to which she can refer. This is a person who has been tired all her life.

Like the hysteric, she may have been been diagnosed with a psychosomatic illness. But the fatigue of hysterics is ambitious: they aim to present a disabled body to the other for privileged care. They expect people to honour their illness, often wearing it like a badge with those close to them, and they seek company in groups of fellow sufferers. In the hysteric, clinicians will discover a complex system of investment that is not present in either the borderline or in a person with a genuine idiomatic somatic debilitation such chronic fatigue syndrome.

The borderline's fatigue is of no interest to her. She does not invest in it, expect others to recognise it, or honour it. She would not even think of joining a group that brought fellow sufferers together. This is because she has no mental conceptualisation that her life could be otherwise. Somatic debilitation is merely the condition of her self-in-the-world.

We find, then, a person who is deeply intermixed with a pain-producing object/other that has the self in a state of constant turmoil.

The borderline contract

Understandably, the analyst may feel confused. Is the other actually causing this pain, or is the patient projecting the negative into the other? In fact, borderline personalities—like perverts—have a unique skill in finding other borderlines with whom they can set up a *borderline contract*. This sets up reciprocal pain festivals in which each causes the other intense distress.

Let's imagine that Penny is a borderline married to Ben, who is also a borderline. Penny allows Ben to go on the mental rampage for hours at a time, perseverating about all the pain she has caused him. She will contest the facts, not in order to solve the problem but merely in order to produce further friction. Penny throws Ben's Sunday newspaper into the bin before he has read it. Ben goes ballistic. Penny does not say she is sorry. She waits until Ben has finished, or she might interrupt him, to instigate a "tit for tat" combat, in which they take it in turns to find bitter fault with each other.

If this is a long-standing relationship, Ben and Penny know exactly which buttons to push in order to produce a constant flow of violent feelings. But they also merge into a *borderline mix* which is the borderline's object of desire: a primary object constructed out of the tatters of turbulence.

They will live together for years, indeed they may remain with one another for life. Once mutually attached, all the libido that might be available for other object relations is directed to this dyadic situation. Their children are not seen as differentiated others who have a life of their own; in the minds of the borderline parents, they are simply part of the toxic mix-up. If they have friends, they will pick fellow borderlines who are usually guaranteed to stir up miserable news for dinner so all of them can engage in a festival of the negative.

Unlike the pervert, however, this is not a situation designed to bring pleasure. The borderline is not cruel to the partner for sadistic reasons, nor is there any masochistic pleasure in submitting to this contract. However, it does enable her to gain an object relation where otherwise there might be none. Her worst fear is she will never find, and merge with, the object of desire. At the end of Melville's *Moby Dick*, Captain Ahab (the quintessential borderline) finally catches the whale. Or rather—and this is the delicious part—Moby Dick finds Ahab. Who is seeking whom? The climax of the novel lies not in the tragic deaths caused by their meeting, but in the fact that at last they each find the object of their love, merge, and go down together. The novel, full of desperately sad characters, ends not with grief but with a kind of frothy celebration of death–love.

Split by the other

It is a commonplace in the analytical literature to focus on how the borderline splits both ego and object into fragments. This is certainly true. Calm self states are sometimes available to this personality, for example when she is at work doing ordinary tasks, because the primary objects in the infant's world will at times have provided adequate care. But while she is apparently functioning normally, she is in fact living with an internal split that fits into the environment in a neutral sort of way. She will tend to work in a sort of decathected haze; meanwhile her mind is actually elsewhere.

Where are her thoughts? Within her split ego, she is quietly feeding off the negative. A colleague might notice her clenching her fists or kicking a dustbin, and assume that she is troubled by a work-related issue, whereas in fact she has travelled down memory lane and is kicking a parent or a sibling, or she is looking forward to bashing her partner that evening.

Klein's view, in part correct, is that the borderline splits the object through vectors of love and hate. In this way, like Freud with his fusion of instinct theory, Klein imagines the self as living in a vacuum with only gestural reference to the actual other. But the borderline's object relations can, in my view, only be understood as a crisis in relation to what Winnicott termed the "environment mother". He pointed out that the good enough mother is both object and environment. As the object mother, she stands for a person; she gives things to the baby and takes them back, she is corporeal, identifiable, and responsible. As the environment mother she is not an individual, she is the world that surrounds the infant. So if a light fixture goes "bang" the infant feels this as a maternal failure.

To my way of thinking, the borderline personality is split not only because she splits the object, but, more relevantly, because she has been split by the environment mother. She will then believe unconsciously that intimacy is achieved through mutual splitting. In this way, borderlines become experts in a kind of choreography in which parts of the self are projected into parts of the other, while at the same time the other is openly invited to do the same.

If the individual were operating in a vacuum, this might seem like the evacuation of the self into the object. However, that would be the case only if the other did not reciprocate. Borderline intimacy is predicated on living in a particular sort of dyad, a relationship in which both participants split as they have been split.

It is important to bear in mind that the function of the environment mother is not always fulfilled by the mother as an individual. The qualities of the environment mother may, for example, be conveyed by a family atmosphere contaminated by rage or frustration. This can infiltrate the infant's world so that the only objects to which she can feel connected are negative ones. Some infants are raised in homes where there is so much conflict that however skilled the object mother (or father as object mother) might be, the environment mother—the infantile world—is overwhelmingly fragmented and violent.

The infant's emotional investment in objects involves a process of receptivity. If the mother loves the infant's smile, the infant will smile because she is receiving the object of her desire—the attention of the mother. If the mother reacts aggressively when the infant is enraged, then the infant will elaborate her angry feelings. So if the family is in a state of extreme duress then the infant will cathect this negative intensity.

It will be seen, however, that this description lacks a psychodynamic explanation. Indeed, the history of the psychoanalytic description of the borderline tends to reveal lists of attributes rather than dynamic exploration. I think this may be because the borderline person professes no need for any dynamic other than the one she has chosen. She remains attached to a ghost-object (the mother as borderline affect), and there has been no forward progress into the world of conflicting forces, affects, ideas, and memories. Such discrete psychic elements are enmeshed with one another with the sole aim of sustaining the shadow of the mother.

Cathecting the abstract object

How do we cathect an abstract quality such as an affect? How do we engage with an abstract object? And how do we relate to an emotion that is a concoction of family life?

This brings us to a crucial characteristic of the analysis of the borderline: she will be unwilling to speak in specific detail about lived experiences, and will prefer to talk about life in the abstract. In a typical session she will begin by saying that her day sucked, that life is always the same, then she will talk about the effect on her of some annoying person at work, but without supplying details.

To some extent, focusing on the disorganising negative object is an organising experience, because the borderline is alienated by any potential space that offers the self an opportunity for some form of unconscious creativity. Potential space is experienced as a black hole. For the borderline, the clinical space can be an unbearable prospect in which the freedom offered by the free associative process is experienced as a dangerously unregulated domain. Even though borderlines, like all people, can and do free associate and could therefore learn from their own unconscious, they experience the relation to that unconscious as impossible.

This dimension makes the analyst's task most complicated. On the one hand the borderline's other is the very turmoil she creates, and such chaotic self experience demonstrates the absence of self-regulating behaviours. She does not pay attention to time, she does not know what is happening during the week, and does not plan ahead. Bills pile up, the ordinary demands of living (maintaining the house, buying school uniforms, getting the car serviced) are not foreseen and nothing is organised in advance.

If a hysteric behaved in the same way, it would generally be driven by an unconscious dynamic aim: the wish to remain a child in an adult's world. Hysterics have all the abilities to self-regulate, but the bliss of being provided for is too pleasurable for them to bother with the everyday grind. They seek instead a form of metaphysical partnership with others in a world that is supposed to transcend the corporeal and material realities of life.

The borderline has no such aim. Self regulation never occurs to her, and life's practicalities are cast aside as if they have no meaning. Indeed, a clinical session is alienating precisely because a potential space offers the possibility of episodic coherence, in which she might understand something from the unconscious. But that form of knowing both acknowledges, and operates within, a generative object relation of self with other.

The analyst who encourages the borderline to free associate may find at first that the patient actually does not know what is being asked of her.

Such a request calls for a type of attention to detail that seems to her utterly superfluous. It is in the grand tragic themes of her life that she finds her objects. They enable her to sustain the only organising thing she knows: endless pain derived from the constancy of bad objects. It is not simply that the analyst's requests to be more specific fall on deaf ears; they can appear to the borderline to be a form of evasion on the analyst's part. To her it seems almost as if the analyst is afraid of living in her preferred realm of free floating abstractions that have been energised but not embodied.

So Ben might say: "I don't want to talk anymore about how she fails me. I have had enough. Last night was the same as always. She was totally insensitive to my needs. She just pisses me off. And if she comes back to me with any of her own stuff I am going to give her the same treatment."

In this account it is not at all clear what exactly has happened. All we know is that Penny fails him generically and that last night was a repeat of this. We do not know what it was that Ben needed, and in what way she was insensitive, or why. We do not know why he thinks she makes him angry, or why he is giving up.

But that is the point. We are not meant to know the specifics. For the borderline, lived experience is a form of corporeality suitable for a kind of blood sucking, as life is abstracted into undefined forms that haunt self and other in a malignant metaphysical universe. If the analyst seeks details he will become the object of fury: "You don't understand. The details aren't important." For this person, it has to do with essences, with truths that have inhabited the other and that permeate the lived space. The details are not relevant because they cannot be found. Indeed, they were never known or knowable.

The borderline, then, lives in a world without psychic corporeality. There is no substance to her discourse, because the wish is to connect to the abstracted forces that were present in the beginning. Any evolved continuity that develops into something substantial is a betrayal of her origins. Therapists can find themselves with a sinking feeling: the borderline will just keep endlessly going over the same old thing. And this is because the patient has a need to remain in a specific realm.

This can seem similar to the hysteric's wish to remain outside the maturational process. However, while the hysteric is devoted to a desexualised universe in which sex is compensated for by a highly narrated, specific discourse-as-body, the borderline trades in ephemera. Although such ghostly presentations may irritate the clinician, it is important to see that borderline relating is in fact deeply devotional. It is all too easy to be critical of the borderline as evasive, evacuative and tricky—they do avoid real contact—but in reacting this way they remain connected to another world, the world from which they came, the world to which they return each day after the session.

The analyst is in a dilemma, and it is interesting to see how many clinicians are, unconsciously, not prepared to "live" in a borderline world without protest. The patient says: "So it didn't work for me yesterday. After work, you know, the same kind of thing happened again, and I just felt fed up." The analyst might reply: "So that was upsetting."

In this exchange, at no point has it been established what the "it" was that did not work for the patient. The details are not sought because this would remove the analyst from the borderline predicament, and he is meant to live with the borderline objects. There is little definition to the figures and events in the patient's life. What is overwhelmingly apparent, however, is that she seems affectively evocative. Indeed, this very abstraction seems to be a necessary vehicle for the borderline's definition of her objects according to the self's affective fury.

Affect is the other

The borderline's affect, then, is the other. The attributes and circumstances of the actual other towards whom the affect is discharged are irrelevant to their function as an abstraction. Herein lies a memory of the beginnings of life, when the object-mother was displaced by abstract dimensions never corporealised, thus never objectified, but seepingly invasive of the self to the point of merger.

In normal development, sensory skin-ego contact with the mother will mingle over time with the infant's nascent body states to form a body sense. In the borderline no such body formation occurs. Instead, affect-states (irritation, anxiety, rage) evoked by the mother, or conjured by the infant to be the body of the mother, fill in for generative sensory experiencing. Non-specific, allegoric, these self-states eventually form the body of a mother whose abstract presence is concealed by the intensity of the child's cathexis of the other.

By working with this kind of object relating, and not challenging the personification of allegorical states by asking for a more detailed report, the therapist implicitly accepts the condition of borderline life. This helps him to see that when the patient is irritated, ranting, feeling damaged by the other, her negative emotions are allegories. They stand for more discrete truths that have to be embedded in a narrative, removed from actual experience, in order to allow her to choose people into whom *allegoric experience* can be projected and personified. In this respect, at least, they seek to find a human other with whom they can have some form of relationship.

This may be a good way to begin work with the borderline. Just as with the narcissist, it is important for the analyst to be a self object and not to impose difference upon the patient. Ultimately, though, it is through asking for the details of lived experience that the analyst helps the patient to corporealise the world. If she is able to start to do this, she may find a route for emerging from the borderline world, relinquishing a kind of ghostland that exists only to infuriate.

A bridge for the borderline

What does it mean to a borderline to detail the traumas of the everyday? What does it mean to *specify*?

In a sense, this is part of the work of unconscious creativity that is inherent in the ego. By asking for details, the analyst facilitates the patient's formation of objects. An abstraction of the other is the other stripped of its specific identity, like a mother who was too confusing to have integrity. As the analyst asks for detail he is therefore helping the borderline to construct the environment mother.

This building of a world is accomplished in a very different way from those analytic approaches that consider the interpretation of borderline splitting as ultimately curative. Though such interpretations certainly form a valued part of the work, it is only apt when directed at the object mother. Interpretation of defensive activities in relation to a single object misses the reality that much of the borderline's mental pain comes from life lived in a world irradiated by environmental rage. The fact that the rage also exists within the borderline herself should not obscure the reality that she was surrounded from the start by the rage in the family.

Returning to our concept of allegorisation, the borderline infant cannot find the object mother but she experiences an environment mother who stirs the self up into madness. Medieval writers would portray aspects of human personality through the creation of allegorical characters, who would each embody a single characteristic such as envy, sloth, or greed. The borderline infant's discontinuous states of anxiety, irritation, rage, and so on, cannot be linked specifically to the object mother, but they are imposed on the infant from her experience of the world. To find an other upon whom these allegories of self can be projected, and in whom they can be personified, is the object relational aim of the borderline.

By asking her to free associate, simply to talk in detail about the events of the day, the analyst helps her to embody her environment. Borderlines tend to get themselves into a catch-22: their social lives consist of hanging out with fellow borderlines, creating a mish mash of "well I am only reacting to you" object relations. In order to move out of this world, they may have to leave behind the partners and others with whom they have been inhabiting it.

It is only when this stage has been accomplished that the analyst can start to focus on the dynamics of the borderline's internal world. It is then more feasible for her to see how she splits off unwanted parts of her personality and projects them into internal objects. If Ben and Penny separate, then when Ben persists in going on about how awful she was, it becomes possible and meaningful for the analyst to think with Ben about the parts of himself that he has been putting into Penny.

Borderline mourning

Inevitably, however, such development involves a painful process of *borderline mourning*. For the whole of her life the borderline's core self has been embedded in affective turmoil that is the outcome of life lived with the primary object. Although the increased sanity achieved through analysis pays psychic dividends that the borderline does appreciate, there is also bereavement over the loss of tempests. There is also a change in mental structure. Whereas previously the other was the personification of allegorical self states, now the borderline is left with no object towards whom this projective-personification can take place.

Jeremy, a borderline, was married to June, also a borderline. Like all borderline relations, their days were characterised by intense explosions on the part of one or both. Respites from conflict were appreciated—without them they would have driven each other mad—but the need to fight and stir up intense fields of hate always defeated the peaceful interludes. After some years of analysis, Jeremy was able to confront June. He asked that she no longer wake him up in the middle of the night because she had something on her mind that could not wait until the morning. Some months later, he told her that it was no longer acceptable for her to throw things, punch the wall, slam doors, or yell at him.

Jeremy was able to get to this point only after he had understood that he took pleasure in June's outbursts because her misbehaviours allowed him to project disturbed parts of himself into her. He had been using her as his own shithouse. It took several years of analysis before he could do this. But for June, who was fortunately also in analysis, this change was not easy to take. Although she found such newly established laws and boundaries helpful, in that she was now able to enjoy some peace of mind, she felt that she and Jeremy were not as close as they had been.

She was right. When she complained that she was no longer able to be her real self in his presence, Jeremy was able to say that he knew that, but that those parts of her that had caused conflict now had to be contained within herself. June countered by pointing out equally egregious dimensions of Jeremy's real self and he accepted that he too would have to contain these aspects of himself.

Both Jeremy and June found this period of new insight very hard to bear. While they appreciated that it did bring some peace of mind and improved relatedness, increased self containment is accomplished at the expense of *borderline intimacy*, which is actually a toxic affective enmeshment.

Motivation for help

Ultimately, the motive for this difficult transformation from borderline intimacy to self containment and new object relatedness is *borderline pain*. The self's stormy entanglement with the world does not result in discovery of the object-mother. Struggle after struggle, wasted relation after wasted relation, do not produce mutual psychic perception. The borderline self lives in a world of fragments, violently saturated with an in-mix of the emotional furies of self and other. As time passes, mental anguish increases. All along there has been an unconscious wish that as long as the self remains attached to the environment-object, eventually the object-mother will emerge and the storm will end. Finally she will be there, ready to help, providing creative objects and introducing the self to generative intimacy.

Borderline relations are consoling as they offer the traces of a relationship, but ultimately they exhaust the couple and lead to unbearable mental pain. To protect the self against the unbearable, the borderline splits the self and the object, projecting the idealised and the despised parts into different containers. Her calm, functioning self may come to the fore when she experiences an object as benign—when she is out shopping, perhaps, or chatting with the postman, or doing tasks at work. These relations relieve her temporarily of the feeling that she is being tossed about at sea. But these are shallow connections that lack depth because their primary purpose is to provide relational forms of asylum. The borderline cannot sustain this sort of split with anyone who is close, or in a situation where there is conflict.

Most of the objects in the borderline universe are bad objects, often the detritus of actual conflicts in lived experience with primary others. The residue of such strife must be contained somewhere, and if the memory leads to too much mental anguish it will be displaced into some bad object or other. So let's imagine that Ben is suffering unbearable memories of the slings and arrows cast his way by Penny and he has reached the point of not being able to bear the agony of these memories. He might unconsciously displace Penny by becoming obsessed with the evils of American foreign policy in Iraq, or with global warming. His psychoanalyst, following his lines of thought, might see that Ben has projected the conflict with Penny into another arena, and by doing so has removed the self from a situation that is existentially more unbearable.

Borderline depression

The problem is, however, that such projection eventually begins to break down precisely because it is a displacement. It involves the use of a borrowed object. Even if Ben's mental anguish has lessened, he will gradually lose interest in these issues as the energy of the projection ceases to be viable. As this happens, he begins to experience *borderline depression*.

This is a type of depression specific to this personality. It appears when the self realises that objects meant to contain the unwanted are ceasing to function, not because the object goes away (global warming is still there) but because the borderline's sense of authenticity starts to disqualify this projective identification. However much she might find respite by blowing off steam, she is drawn inexorably towards actual combat with present others.

This withdrawal from the negative objects is rather like the sea's withdrawal before a tsunami. The water recedes from the object world because it is being drawn in to form a huge wave that will destroy everything in its path. And those who work with, live with, or witness the borderline will see this in action: after a period of apparent calm, she suddenly goes on a rampage of highly destructive behaviour.

Many of the alcoholics or drug addicts who are in 12-step programmes are borderline personalities seeking a type of container that will encourage them towards good behaviour. The group and the mentors are the good objects, the alcohol or the drug is the bad object, and for some weeks or months the borderline might be able to accept this construct. But she will then go on a rage-filled binge. This is the psychic tsunami that crashes through barriers and boundaries, and violates the order of things.

Borderline depression, then, is a despair about ever being able to leave the object of attachment, of ever being able to give up enmeshment with the negative. The depression is almost always anticipatory. In the days before the self's abandonment of good behaviour there is a depressive realisation that she is about to fail, a kind of premonition of psychic self-abandonment in which the self knows that it will give up the battle to leave the negative object.

Understandably, this may be a time of suicide risk for the borderline. She knows that once again she is on a hazardous and terrifying journey that will inevitably take her right back to the primal origins of the self's existence.

Psychotic coldness

There is a particular *coldness* that can be seen across the spectrum of character disturbances. This coldness is the freezing of the self with the aim of destroying all cathexes of the object. Often, the other does not know this is taking place. It is not equivalent to killing off the object as it is intended to communicate a form of hate that the self has towards the other.

The narcissist's coldness is an affective statement: "You have differed from me, so I leave you out in the cold." The borderline's coldness: "You and I are not one. This leaves me cold but I am recovering through hot rage." The schizoid's coldness: "I am frozen and cannot be warmed, so go away." The manic-depressive: "I withdraw into the deep freeze of depression where I become the Ice-God." The schizophrenic: "I am not an I. I cannot hear you." The paranoid: "My cool innocence freeze-frames your veniality."

The borderline feels cold fury, and she aims to project this into the other, who will then become enmeshed in her primary object relation. In marital disputes, for example, she will withdraw into prolonged remove from her partner. However hard he may try to reach her, however angry he may get, nothing seems to faze her. In defeating the other's efforts, she gradually reduces him to nothing—in other words, to the same state that she herself inhabits. Borderline coldness, then, serves to create relational friction that will ignite constant heated debates, producing material for further dispute, the fuel for discord.

At this point I shall illustrate further the distinction between the cold rage of the narcissistic and that of the borderline. First the narcissist.

Howard is married to Juliet. They argue most of the time. On occasion Juliet pins Howard to the wall with an irrefutable accusation. Howard has failed to do the dishes even though he promised to do them two hours ago. She points to her watch and reminds him of the time. Howard stops talking and walks out of the room. Juliet follows and throws a book at him and then leaves the house, slamming the front door. Some time later she returns, but she does not see Howard and they do not speak to one another for an hour. She starts to panic, wondering whether he is still there. She races through all the rooms and finds him in a remote part of the house. "What are you doing here?" she asks. Howard says, "Not much." She asks if he would like to go for a walk but he doesn't reply. Juliet asks if he is still upset. Howard says, "No," but his voice is sarcastic and his face signifies fury.

In analysis, this manoeuvre becomes clear: when Howard is furious with the analyst he withdraws into cold silence. What the analyst understands is that, by resorting to a sign system, Howard is refusing the signifying function of language and opting instead for a preverbal form of communication. Speech is now used solely in order to have a disturbing effect on the other.

Narcissistic coldness forces the analyst to be out in the cold—alone, without a sentient other. In doing this the narcissist recreates an environment derived from his primary encounters with the world. Beset by an uneven environmental situation, he freezes the object world and creates an ice-kingdom of ideal objects. This is "The Winter's Tale": statues replace the living.

The borderline will attempt to utilise this coldness but it will not work. Within a dispiritingly short period of time, cold rage will turn to overt hot rage. The borderline's coldness is almost a wished-for accomplishment, a developmental aim. If only the object of rage could be put on ice. However, periods of wilful coldness do allow the self to find temporary respite from conflict. When this occurs in analysis and the borderline is freezing out the analyst, the discovery of respite may be transformative.

Anxiety

Narcissistic rage is in fact a concealed anxiety attack; it is aimed solely at restoring the self's equilibrium. The narcissist has no inclination to punish the object as an end in itself. His behaviour may appear sadistic but he does not derive pleasure from exacting revenge. He is angry in order to rid the self of the destabilising effects of the causes of anger, as well as discharging the anger itself. With the borderline, the rage *is* the primary object and she escalates it in order to intensify the object relation. Like the narcissist, the borderline does not derive sadistic pleasure from her states of rage.

Axioms that constitute the logic of the borderline character

1. I do not have an originating sense of who I am, but I can feel a "me" that is formed out of reaction to a disturbing other.
2. To keep that sense of me going I must continually find disturbing others.

3. When an actual other is not available I must evoke disturbing thoughts, feelings, and memories in order to create the shape of the disturbing other.
4. In the beginning the disturbing object seems to be "on the outside". I have no ideas about it, but if I can react to it then these reactions mesh with the object and become one with it.
5. I am not an "I" but a "me", created as the wake of the other's disruption. I am the turbulence of the other, attached as its after-effect.
6. To form a relation with anyone (as I am not an "I" but a "me-after-the-you") I must disturb others so that I can find my place and become what it is possible for me to become.
7. If you try to help me get better, to think clearly and to become an independent person, you are trying to kill me and I shall have to defeat you.
8. I will turn your good efforts into persecutors that I mirror back to you as harmful actions that confuse you. Then we are together and in this way I allow you to be with me.
9. I choose turbulence. It is the only object to which I can be attached and which reflects a sense of me.

Psychoanalysis of the borderline

Over the last fifty years, more essays and books have been written on the treatment of the borderline personality than on any other character type. Writers from almost all schools of analysis have emphasised the need to bear the assaults of the borderline, and this is certainly the case. However, I differ in some respects from other analysts in that I believe borderlines *are* capable of thinking about themselves objectively. This means that it is possible to interpret the logic of their character as outlined above, but in doing so the analyst must anticipate a ferocious attempt on the part of the patient to deny that such interpretation makes sense. In this respect, recent conceptualisations of mentalization are eagerly embraced by the borderline (and by many analysts who treat them) because it lets both participants off the hook of this intense object relation.

Harking back to the days of ego psychology in the mid-1950s, mentalization theory was seen as dividing the psychic world into the haves and the have-nots. At that time, borderline patients (and some others) were considered too disturbed, to suffer from too much deficiency in early ego formation, to be able to understand interpretation of their dynamics. Indeed, interpretation was dangerous as it could precipitate ego regression through release of primary process thinking. Instead, the patient's defences should be shored up in "supportive psychotherapy". This meant that the analyst would go so far and no further in analysing this person who was thought be unanalysable.

A different division is proposed by the advocates of mentalization. They maintain that interpretation does not impose an ego regression; it is simply that these people cannot use interpretation to conceputualise what is being said to them. In other words, say what you will, they do not get it.

My own clinical experience does not support this theory. Ironically, indeed, the deficit view mirrors the psychology of maternal disinterest: the patient is so lacking in ability that she cannot be given the full-on presence of an other who engages the self. However well-intentioned this approach, it unwittingly consolidates borderline personality structure and is an unknowing act of abandonment. It can also be seen as defensive, protecting the participants from the anxiety of psychic change.

Members of the "old" Kleinian group, such as Rosenfeld, never divided people into the haves and the have-nots. All analysands could expect to meet with analytical interpretation: that is, with the effort to put character and its movement in the transference into language. Uncovering the psychodynamics of the borderline—the choice of turbulent object relations and the reasons for this—enables the analyst to interpret this to the patient. Although this interpretation will be powerfully resisted, there will be unmistakable signs of the relief that comes with the realisation she does have a true self, however much it may have been dislodged or seemingly eradicated by history and psychic events.

In the course of time, at moments when the patient is detached from the borderline object of desire and there are periods of quiet, she will start to be able to listen to her free associations. This allows both participants to attend to non-borderline, non-conflictual issues, in other words, the everyday differentiated elements of life become available for thought.

CHAPTER 3

The Manic Depressive

A problem we face in thinking about a person who suffers from manic depression is that the term "bipolar" is now commonly used in its place. As so often happens, once a term is adopted as popular jargon, the subtle defining characteristics of the disturbance can become lost and simplified through a kind of mass marketing. As a consequence, many people are now termed "bipolar" who have never had a manic episode in their life.

The true specificity of diagnostic categories becomes clear when we meet a person who is either manic depressive or schizophrenic. These are people who endure real mental suffering. There is no mimetic representation of suffering, as we find in hysteria, nor is there the pursuit of the negative for a festival of bad mental states, as there is with the borderline. The manic depressive and the schizophrenic are without a doubt people who have been victimised by mental distress that is at times terrifying to watch.

Basics

Setting aside the question of aetiology, a person is manic-depressive when he oscillates between extreme highs and extreme lows of mood. I emphasise extreme. We all have ups and downs, and we all have the potential for manic and depressive swings—hence the mass marketing of the term "bipolar". The same is true of the elements that constitute the borderline, the hysteric, the schizoid, and others. We all have elements of these character disorders within us. The manic depressive, however, is as far removed from the ordinary highs and lows of life as Bruckner's music is from Corelli's.

From a psychoanalytical perspective, what are the core structural elements of the manic depressive? If we bear in mind that from this person's point of view the deepest suffering resides in the long periods of profound depression, then we may see that the manic mood is unconsciously sought as a form of liberation from the oppression of depression. Typically, something happens in his life that triggers the shift from depression to mania. It may be an exciting event or some form of success, or it might be as simple as meeting a new person who is particularly interesting. There is always a specific stimulating event and close examination of the history of any manic episode will reveal this.

Why is this important?

Taking a history

Let us think for a moment about the ironic consequences of what we may think of as a sociocultural collusion with the anti-historical position of the manic depressive.

This character disorder is viewed as a "disease" that is self-defining, rather as someone might be suffering from a virus. This encourages clinicians to move immediately to the biological side of the situation, often discovering hereditary factors in the history of the patient, and medication may become the preferred form of treatment.

Too often there is little attention given to the history of the manic depressive self, and because of this a vital therapeutic agency is lost. In my experience, it is crucial to effective analytical work that the clinician take a detailed history in order to help the patient connect the events in his life that evoked his state of mind. This is far more important with the manic depressive than with most other patients.

When the life events around the onset of both the mania and the depression are examined in microscopic detail, this history-taking process is in itself therapeutically enhancing. This is because in a manic epsiode the fabric of the self's memory is shredded. The person's history, context, relationships and obligations are cast aside. He becomes immediately ahistorical and completely uninterested in the immediate context of his euphoria. Questions about when he began to feel this way, where he was, and what had been happening may be treated by him at best with impatience and most often with contempt, dismissed as the mundane detritus of the ordinary. But if the clinician persists—"well, humour me then"—he may be able to find links between the external and intrapsychic events in the pre-manic period and the onset of the manic episode.

In addition to the importance of this information in making sense of the manic epsiode, the work of history-taking in itself slows the episode down under the weight of recollection. It roots the analysand in the everyday and implicitly works against his transcendent contempt for everyday life. Also, by returning the analysand to the context of his mania, the analyst facilitates the return of split-off depressive realities. This aspect is crucial, as it reduces both the intensity and the vectorisation of mania.

Affliction

The manic patient dismisses the relevance of the everyday because of his grandiose frame of mind. When he subsequently becomes depressed, he lacks interest in the events of his life for a different reason: because the self is caught up in a depression that destroys meaning. The person who is deeply depressed feels he is afflicted by something that has taken over the self. There is a profound sense of loss of agency and a sort of sacrificial capitulation to depression as a punishment of the self.

Like the manic person, the depressed individual is reluctant to return to the moment when he became depressed. Both states of mind carry psychic innoculations against the work of insight. But in both mania and depression, when he is returned to the context of the change of mood, what may have seemed like a meaningless swing of biological processes becomes painfully meaningful.

Indeed, the central characteristic of the manic depressive's strategy is to avoid unbearable meaning. The strategy of avoidance—stunningly colluded with by the biological approach to mental health—aims to concretise the self's situation in order to avoid examination of his lived experience. For it is in these details that the investigating clinician will find a complex of internal and external relations that has woven a fabric of profound pain.

Powers of thought

If the self, early on, lives in an environment in which mental pain is linked to disturbing environmental circumstances, then the person will value thought and the search for meaning. But if the manic depressive grew up in a family culture that was uninterested in personal history and existential meaning, when he has a breakdown no thought will be given to psychological phenomena.

One of the startling features of this thoughtlessness is that manic individuals are in other respects often remarkably full of ideas. So how do we understand this apparent lack of interest in their own personal psychology? Why is the psychological so readily displaced onto the biological?

To understand this paradox, we need to see how this person behaves when in a manic state. The psychiatric literature is full of references to how people who are manic are full of "loose associations", they produce a "word salad". I took this as gospel truth until I started to work with my first manic depressive patients in analysis. When they were manic they would speak at remarkable speed, jumping from topic to topic, but I discovered to my surprise that if I carried on listening and did not give up on them, I began to see that they were actually free associating. The associations appeared "loose" because their speech was not obviously consciously coherent, but as I listened it was possible to discover that they were in fact pursuing clear lines of thought.

Therapeutic slowing down

To attend to these sequences of thought, however, I found I needed to slow the patients down. This was not easy. I would often have to interrupt the flow of ideas and ask them to be quiet so that I could speak. (In my experience, manic patients invariably comply with this, for reasons we shall explore later.)

I was frequently taken by the brilliance of their thinking and, as honesty is the best policy in the work of being a psychoanalyst, I would say that I found their thoughts quite remarkable. I believe this had the effect of allowing them to feel appreciated but also puzzled. What had they said that was so brilliant? I could then point out to them how they seemed to be working on quite specific themes, and since I was drawing attention to the exact words they themselves had spoken, the grandiose side of their personality would be persuaded that I was not simply to be dispelled.

Time and again I would do this. And time and again we would look at the previous 15 minutes and examine what they had been working on. This was a way of slowing up the manic process to *think* about what was being delivered up at breakneck speed. As they grew accustomed to working in this way, they came to expect that their mania would be slowed down, and also that there would probably be mood swings during the session. They would come in manic; I would slow them down. I was therefore the depressive element. They made room for me and I made room for them. In effect, both sides of the manic-depressive split were in the room together.

Colleagues hearing my presentation of these sessions almost invariably had the same response. They would complain of feeling flooded by what they heard, they felt unable to make links, they would feel they were being attacked or their minds disabled, and so on. It seemed that many of them had long since given up on following these patients' lines of thought.

Was there a hint here of the aetiology of this illness?

The background

Imagine yourself as a child. You have an idea—or maybe two or three. You speak them and your parents hear your words, but they are preoccupied—present physically but not mentally—and they find you a bit too much. They have other things to do. Father may be reading the paper as he does every night. Mother is cleaning up after dinner and tidying the house for the next day. As time passes your "talkings" come to be looked upon as things-in-themselves. It is not what you say but the fact that you are saying something that becomes the phenomenon. No one is listening because no one has the time.

The child's mind then races faster to try to prove more entertaining. Eventually it does not matter who is listening—indeed, the other may not even be there anymore. For the child, it is sometimes enough that these moments of inspiration and instinctual excitement become the source of the pleasure, irrespective of the absent response. But if his attempts to offer these excitations to the parents repeatedly fail, eventually a cycle is established: excitation, a failed attempt to communicate it, then despair over the absence of the other.

So if we draw a parallel with contemporary mental health approaches, we might ask: how many manic depressives are listened to? How many therapists "treat" them rather than talking with them?

Writing of the schizoid, Winnicott suggested that in this case the mind itself becomes the object. Corrigan and Ellen-Gordon also wrote of the "mind-object". As a child, the manic person too has to turn to the mind as an object, because the mind will listen to him whereas the human other will not. Thus an early split develops in the self between a speaking portion and a listening portion. The listening portion is an assumed other, but not a differentiated one. Because the actual human others did not provide a paradigm of listening, the manic depressive does not actually listen to what he says, but instead puts in place a kind of listening dummy, so that the mind can speak even if no answer is to be forthcoming.

Analytical interruption and differentiated listening

When the analyst interrupts the manic patient's speaking, she is both known and unknown. He assumes that the other is absorbed by his discourse, but in fact the other is so absorbed as to have long since disappeared. The parents were of no use because they failed to listen, so the listener had to be replaced by a purely intrapsychic function. When the analyst speaks as a true separate other, interested in what is being said, she is a rather uncanny embodiment of that internal function. So for the patient it is more than a surprise when she pays attention.

But the attentive analyst has a competitor. In the strange oedipal configuration of the manic depressive the analyst's listening competes with a narcissistic other that is a part of the self. It exists in order to rid the self of any need for an external other. When the analyst demonstrates differentiated listening, even proving over time that she is in fact more attentive to what is being said than the speaker himself, a crisis develops in the analysis of the manic depressive.

The arrival of a differentiated listener is shocking and must be resisted with enormous force. This is because the mind has been re-structured around the paradigm of absence rather than presence. Other has long since been subsumed into self, so when the other speaks he feels, understandably, that his entire psychic structure (a compensatory defence) has been undermined. This experience is akin to the loss of relatedness. These personalities have incorporated relatedness into psychic structure in a very particular way: they exist in relation to themselves, and to themselves alone.

Analyst as "love object"

This sort of work is very slow. (The analyst who does not enjoy being patient might as well give up working with the psychotic personality.) Eventually, however, the analyst's ability to survive the manic person's destruction of her comments becomes a love object. It is hard to put it any other way.

In the manic stage my patients would sometimes pound the wall, hit themselves on the head, or scream, "Okay, go ahead and speak then!" Or they might go rigid on the couch in protest. Even though I may have felt intimidated, sometimes frightened, I would speak in a calm voice and say what I thought. As the months and years passed, it became clear that my capacity to remain myself, in the face of the analysand's depersonalising representation of me as a mere object, gradually affirmed for them that they were with a human other.

Along with this there would be the development of a particular type of love in the transference. For a long time, my relentless presence, together with my willingness to be destroyed, would seem amusingly boring. It was as if I was a kind of steady state—especially when the analysand was manic. But my position constituted a middle way, mood wise, as I was working with both the manic and the depressive aspects of their existence, always making links to the mentally troubling features of their life. However, when these patients began to shift out of their radical mood swings, this was not through identification with me.

It was through experience of my *effect*, internalised and structuralised, that they found me inside them as an element of difference.

I ceased to be an empty other, the cipher with whom they had grown accustomed to living, and became instead a recognisable actual other who was listening to what they said. The knowledge that I derived from what they articulated, especially during their manic moments, ultimately became a shared body of knowledge. Until then there had been no listening other, and therefore no internal correlate for a listening other.

Without memory

The result of such absence is an inability to store the self's own experiencings and sayings. Manic personalities therefore have virtually no personal memory of what they have experienced, and they will often rely upon myths and legends as substitute forms of recollection. At the best they retain crowning accomplishments or apparently definitive moments of despair. In effect they have manic-depressive memory points: extreme highs and lows.

The rootlessness of this personality has much to do with the absence of memory and a deficit of specific personal knowledge. In the absence of a firm sense of his own existence, he substitutes a striking grandiosity. Compensating from early in life for the absence of ordinary celebration of the self, he will have only his grandiose recollections. Memory of our lives—especially unconscious memory—is the background to any self. The collecting of memories is a mental capability that perceives and stores our lived experiences. It is a matrix that perceives our reality and organises many things, not least our dreams, our reveries, and our personal creativities, and it contributes to our capacity for intimate sharing with the other.

In the manic state, memory feels like trivia in comparison to the self's grandiloquent observations and declamations. In the depressed state, it is almost impossible to make contact with the history of the self because it feels devoid of meaning. In both phases the manic depressive lives caught in a vicious circle, as a self without memory is not only rootless and rudderless. He is unconsciously dropped as a love object.

We often think of memory and nostalgia as closely linked. When we "go down memory lane" it is often with a certain kind of love or affection for what we recollect—people, places, our prior selves. But looked at from another perspective, memory is also a part of us that loves our self. We are commemorated by our unconscious. Think of the person who suddenly recollects with delight something that has been lost for decades. It is as if he has been given a gift. We sense that our unconscious looks after us; it is the mother to our self. So to have a memory is to be loved by this internal mother.

Manic depressive personalities struggle to retrieve discrete memories and this absence sustains an internal conviction that they are not loved. In place of this internal nurturing there are moments of self adoration, as an attempt to make up for the loss of love by means of grandiose claims. The self is the next Messiah. Intriguingly enough, manic personalities do not require validation of their claims from any actual other. They seek witnessing but not confirmation. It is enough that someone is present to hear or overhear them. Apart from this, they demand silence.

Becoming God

For them, the only good other is an object. Human otherness has been destroyed by the experience of subtle forms of neglect in infancy and childhood, and in place of the other the self turns to mind and its products. Without memory of human lived experience, he has no choice but to become a god who has transcended the particular. One can see here something of the brilliant strategy of the manic state. The structure of mythic thought, or of history as legend, means that a self can return to certain points of reference again and again. Because these are so simple they can be remembered, and can serve as a form of container for the self's immediate evacuations.

In ancient cultures myth and legend played a role in creating a sense of transgenerational community, but it may well be that they also provided a way of leaving behind the disturbing experiences (memories) of life in the real. Think of how religions function. Groups get together and over time they imagine divinities. They believe they are looked after by these divine beings, although they are also punished by them. Even when life is at its worst they can believe that these gods-on-high will not forget them. In more euphoric states they can feel themselves close to, or even possessed by, these gods. The point here is that religions function where memory of the ordinary might otherwise have been.

Looked at this way we can see manic depression as a type of cultural inheritance, and how manic depressive "solutions" in fact reflect a very widespread and accepted social practice. We can now see why manic depressive people claim to be Jesus or Moses more often than Shakespeare. The more secular manic depressives may claim to be the President or the King, but rarely will they claim to be Dostoyevsky or Mozart. Their aim is to be someone who rules over human beings from on high.

Ordinary mood swings

Despite the grandiosity of their imaginings, the psychological factors contributing to manic depressive distress may be remarkably undramatic, even ubiquitous. The manic depressive personalities with whom I have worked have all come from families that seem otherwise rather ordinary. The family atmosphere does not seem particularly colourful or toxic, in fact it is usually rather bland and tends to be somewhat depressed.

So what is the problem?

The answer is something of an irony. I believe the families of manic depressives differ in one salient respect from other ordinary families. Most families have visible highs and lows, and as a normal child grows up he will have mood swings: at school, in the home, playing with friends. Going to a scary movie is a mood-swinging event, as is going to a dance, or to church. In other words, the non-manic depressive population is acculturated to mood swings throughout childhood and adolescence.

In the family of the manic depressive, however, there will typically have been few such swings. The emphasis is on keeping life level. The family members will have certain highs and lows, but these are not sufficiently extreme or frequent to have provided the internal means of metabolising manic depressive episodes.

Bleak house

Although I have offered here some ideas on typical family characteristics, it would be misguided to claim that there is any one individual route to manic depression, or for that matter to schizophrenia. These complex disturbances will insist upon specific adaptations to their enigmatic dimensions. My observation that people who suffer manic depression seem to come from families that are largely inattentive to their internal worlds is also true of many others—from schizophrenia to normopathy and obsessive-compulsive disorders. It is also true of many people who seem free of any particular character categorisation.

The manic depressive mentality may also be related to a split in ordinary childhood states of mind. Most children can feel inadequate at times in the face of the capabilities they witness in the adult world. It is a long, often painfully slow progression from the cognitive skills of the four-year-old to those of the eight-year-old and from there to the fourteen-year-old, and so it goes. Melanie Klein's theory of the depressive position—as a psychic accomplishment in which the infant unconsciously realises that the object of love and of hate are one and the same—does not address other forms of depression-in-waiting. Indeed, the inevitable ego lag between being aware of these new skills-in-waiting and having them in the self's possession imbues children with the feeling that they are always behind the game.

Having themselves been through childhood, adults sense the child's experience of this challenging stage in the life span, so children are repeatedly praised for accomplishments and celebrated in ways that will disappear when they move into young adulthood. These celebrations are necessary anti-depressant medications in the life of the normal child.

In the history of the manic depressive, however, we see the uncelebrated child. This will have produced a type of depression. Although such a child will progress from one school grade to the next, from one stage of development to another, he lives in a world in which the lack of celebration of the self produces a pervasive sense of loneliness and marginality.

On the surface, we see here something of the same picture as with the schizoid personality. However, the schizoid child will replace enlivened participation in the stages of childhood with intense preoccupation with the world of inner imagining. The schizoid may turn towards the world of mathematics, or science, or fiction, or music, in order to find nourishment from a realm that can be containing, reliable, and generative. The manic depressive child, on the other hand, feels only a hopeless sorrow, a fog-like inner state in which the distance of the parents and others feels like an objectification of a hopeless life to come.

It is with this background that he enters adolescence, which suddenly and violently ruptures every axiom he has come to live by. One of the reasons why psychiatry and science believe that manic depression is a genetic disorder is that the biology of adolescence plays a huge role in the formation of this personality. Indeed, one might claim that until adolescence there can be no such condition as manic depression.

No other personality shifts its formation as dramatically in the adolescent era. This is because the emergence of the powerful sexual and aggressive drives intrinsic to the ordinary biological changes of adolescence can appear to this cocooned and reclusive being as gifts from God sent by special delivery. As biology shocks his inner life, new sensations course through the body, galvanising the mind into the production of astonishing new thoughts, ideas, images, and fantasies, the adolescent now feels that he has been rescued by the arrival of inspiration.

It is important to establish that although many manic depressives will proceed to become psychotically delusional, the recognition that they are the guardian-containers of the inspiring is not a delusion to begin with. But just as they struggled to find their place in the psychosocial realm of childhood, they now fail to see how their own personal experience is shared by their fellows. Because they remain cut off from other children, they are unable to share these shifts in their being with playmates and friends. Had they been able to do this, they would have found common ground, and would not have needed to evolve a grandiose platform from which to engage with the world.

It is crucial to understand that the manic person unconsciously experiences the thoughts and fantasies that intoxicate him as deriving from a mind that is itself a sexual organ. As we shall see, this organ is a highly complex condensation of a maternal breast and a phallus that inseminates all forms of generativity. Both idioms of the sexual are magically contained in this person's mental closet.

Early signs

It is striking to see an adolescent who has just had his first manic episode. It is usually an astonishing event, but it appears so extreme in part because it occurs against a backdrop of environmental blandness.

This adolescent will have been seen as rather nerdish and remote. Then one day a smile crosses his face. He might suddenly laugh out loud in class, to the shock of the group. When asked what made him laugh, he says, "Nothing." He keeps grinning, rocking back and forth, sometimes bursting into laughter, and he looks at the others as if to say, "Oh my God ... if you only knew!" Events then happen very quickly. Later that afternoon he is found in the local mall, stripped to the waist, proclaiming to all and sundry that he has the answers to all the world's problems. It is not long before he finds himself in hospital, in the midst of a full-scale manic episode.

Earlier we discussed the fact that manic depressive people have not had experience in processing the ordinary highs and lows of life. When they reach adolescence and hormones kick in they are now sexualised beings, but as the family steady-state has tended towards the depressive, the family ego (so to speak) is not interested in libido. The highs and lows of everyday life are instinctual learning centres in which the instincts can find objects and gain satisfaction, and the self can learn how to live with excitation. Not so in the family of the manic depressive, which prefers a quiet life and is not invested in helping the children with their instincts. So when adolescence brings the first powerful sexual excitations, together with masturbation fantasies, these are profoundly shocking to the child.

The manic depressive adolescent's identification with being a world-saving figure or some kind of god is in part an effort to escape the toxic effects of instinctual life. It is also an effort omnipotently to nullify the specific sexual fantasy that seems about to consign him to hellfire. By becoming Jesus, he aims to escape his body, climbing into a virtual reality created through powerful flights of imagination. And to some extent it works. It removes him from the chaotic experience of sexual excitation and from the confusions of peer group relations, as he is often seen now by others as a disturbing presence. He may even be removed to another school.

Unfortunately this teaches the self that manic flights do temporarily relieve him of something more unbearable. This is one of the great clinical challenges in working with the young manic depressive, because in mania he has found a kind of freedom from a life of blandness. It is a psychic medication that gives the self a high in more respects than one.

He is high in mood, that is for sure, but he is also inhabiting a higher plane than his peers, from whom he becomes separated. This is something of a hidden ambition for the manic depressive who, out of all the various psychotic personalities, is the most likely to embrace his diagnosis. He wears a metaphorical sign saying "manic depressive—do not get too close". As long as the world leaves him alone, the schizoid aspect of this personality is assured a relatively safe passage.

However, this exalted phase does not last. Waiting for the manic person is the inevitable doom of the depressed state. It is impossible to grasp the suffering endured by this person until you see him in the depths of his depression. The image of a Fallen Angel is the representational embodiment of his psychic reality.

The self's depression is like a compressed collage of all the depressing features of his history condensed into the body-self as an iconic protest. It is a cocktail of affects, the most profound of which is anger. This anger is complex. It is directed in the first place against the self, for the false belief that it could escape its depressive fate. It is directed against the world of others, who are experienced as having failed the self. Indeed, the havoc wreaked by the manic person is shocking and those close to him may well have to step back. But of all the objects of such anger the one constant object is the family of origin which is seen as strangling his vitality. The manic depressive will be unable to point to any single feature of a mother or a father that is distinctively cruel or unusual, but the difficulty in locating why he is ill only seems to add to his sense of rage.

It seems apt now to discuss medication. One cannot see suffering like this, in my view, without conceding that this is an occasion in which psychotropic intervention is humane. If it will relieve the suffering, then it should be administered. Nothing is gained by allowing anyone to endure such suffering, and contrary to many psychoanalytical opinions, I believe that this does not interfere with the work of analysis. But medication will not cure the manic depressive; it can only make life more bearable and take the more savage edges off the illness. If one is to help this individual emerge out of the psychology of manic depression then the only solution I know of is intensive long term psychoanalysis.

This work will comprise many clinical tasks and I shall turn to these now.

As we have discussed, the manic depressive's wish to find some way out of the toxicity of excitement has resulted in a form of omnipotence that allows him to be excluded from the group. In analysing this strategy, the analyst will find there is intense resistance to participating in a human relationship. All efforts will be made to idealise the analyst in order to get rid of him. But if the analyst persists in inhabiting his ordinariness, then over time the patient will gradually become part of the fabric of human relatedness. Here, as with schizophrenia, the relationship between analyst and patient is everything. However interpretively gifted the analyst, and however astutely he tracks and interprets the free associations, these efforts will be useless unless an idiom of intimacy can be established between self and other.

As with schizophrenia, the analyst must help this person to see what is ordinary in what appear to be extraordinary states of mind. An example. The patient has been Jesus for a couple of weeks and it feels like the right time to talk about this. It may work for the analyst to say something like, "Well, of course, we all aspire to be Jesus in some way or another." This comment will invite curiosity, questioning, and then mutual exploration of the nature and aims of grandiose thinking.

There are specific difficulties peculiar to the analysis of a manic depressive. One is a particular anal sexual organisation. Some manic depressives are consciously aware, during the manic episode, of a sensation between the anus and the penis or vagina. It will be described in different ways, but usually as a sexual sensation, one that oscillates between the two sexual zones. Work with this particular erotogenic presentation has led to the understanding that there is a sexualisation underlying the manic episode, in which the anus links to the genitals: he is evacuating mental phenomena in order to "fuck" the universe. Anyone working with the manic person will be struck by the astonishing amount of material being verbally downloaded, but it may not be so obvious that there is a corresponding sexualisation of this action. Via this anal–genital axis, the manic depressive feels authorised by a co-operation functioning between two objects that eliminate: the penis (or vagina and urethra) and the anus. This sensation is often accompanied by another one. He will often smack his lips as if he is sucking on something. Sometimes he will literally be sucking his tongue. If this is interrrupted by the analyst, he may stick his tongue violently into his cheek, rather as though he is giving the analyst the finger—a "fuck you" by tongue-in-cheek. This is no ordinary tongue-in-cheek moment, however. The manic depressive is sucking on the productions of the mind as if it were a maternal breast. Sucking on the mind is violent and intense. Although some of the food for thought is verbally expelled through speech, it is as if at the same time an unconscious phantasy operates to eliminate the waste through the anus. The urethra is also activated, creating an anal–urethral connection that generates a genital feeling. The world is now being fucked by manic processes of elimination.

This remarkable internal activity (sucking from the mind, sending verbal food for thought out of the mouth and evacuating the remains out of the anus and urethra, creating a genital sensation) generates in the manic period a psychic sense that the self is indeed some kind of remarkably hermetic god who is feeding the world. As the world is being fed verbal wisdom, the anal area creates compost for the world's organic regeneration. Nothing is wasted.

Encountering this psychosomatic universe is a complex clinical challenge for the psychoanalyst. As always simple observations are better than complex interpretations. It is usually enough to say, "I notice that when you are speaking you smack your lips as if you are sucking on something." In time this can lead to the idea that the patient seems to be sucking on his mind. It is very important that this must not be a pejorative comment but an observation followed by the interpretive understanding that the analysand has found in his mind a loving object that he believes feeds him and makes him feel much stronger.

The underlying anal–urethral–genital axis should not be analysed until the analysand himself makes some kind of reference to it, but when this occurs the analyst might say, "It makes sense to me that as you get these thoughts of yours out by any means, anal or urethral, it feels as if you are now having some divine intercourse with the world."

Manic depressives are like Zeus. They do not need intercourse with the other to procreate—their offspring are born out of the mouth, the anus, the urethra, and the genital. By the logic of inversion, this need for no one means that all others are in need of the manic depressive. Thus there is an intense urgency, bordering on panic, to get the world to recognise its need of him before there is a catastrophe.

The analyst can calmly allude to this: "You feel that the world is in urgent need of what you have to say," or, "It's as if something awful will happen if the world doesn't heed your message." There is an apocalyptic anxiety in the manic depressive that is clinically challenging. At this point, however, he solves a problem that the schizophrenic cannot. For the schizophrenic in the apocalyptic moment, the sky is falling in and he must take cover, often literally hiding under a table or in a closet. But for the manic depressive, apocalyptic panic can be averted by being transferred into motoric activity. He may translate it into a system of active public services: he is the fireman, the policeman, the newspaper editor, the President. He turns himself into a kind of Action Man.

The analyst might say: "I think you feel that a catastrophe is imminent and you are rushing around trying to solve all the problems." This can then lead on to a more direct interpretation: "I think you are panicked because you feel yourself falling into a disaster. You feel you don't know what to do, so you are trying to stem this rather heroically by taking all kinds of action."

The disaster is, of course, the sudden fall into depression. The panic is a warning from the ego that the manic depressive's universe is about to be annihilated. It truly feels like the end of the world. Unlike the schizophrenic, for whom there is no imagined future after annihilation, the manic depressive knows he will go into a hell, a cold, voiceless, visionless world where there is no food for thought. The self will starve. The world cannot be saved. It is all over.

Until the resurrection. For it is a common feature of this depression that the person somewhere holds on to the "light" of the mania. Even if the manic period has meant the destruction of partnerships, friendships, even his professional life, it still feels to him that mania will be the only cure.

In the depressive stage this person has lost something profound: he is mourning the loss of the self that was there during the manic phase. The breast-mind is empty. The body is listless. Sensation and pleasure are gone. Manic-depressive grief has been the subject of many psychiatric and psychoanalytical studies. Two classic essays, Freud's "Mourning and Melancholia" and Klein's "Mourning and its relation to manic depressive states" are the finest writings on this type of mourning, and I shall not reiterate them here. Instead, I want to focus on a type of delusion peculiar to the manic depressive.

As we have seen, in the manic state their influencing machine is the mind–body co-ordinate. In the depressed state that self is still there, but it exists now as *the ghost within*. This is very hard to describe, but it is as if the manic-depressive is a double personality. In the depressive state he holds within him the ghost left behind by the manic body that has zoomed off into the stars, leaving the actual self in the darkness of depression. The relation to this ghost is a profound secret. At times it seems as if the cloak of depression is meant to hide it, to keep it out of sight of the observing other.

No doubt there are many ways to think about this, but in my view it is the ghost of the abandoned infant-child self, now held in hibernation by the depressed and dejected being who had once been cared for by the mind-mother in a life-enhancing way. We see here how the manic depressive's grief aims to protect a potentially definitive death from realisation, keeping the ghost of the past alive through a secret object relation.

This is clinically observable in typical depressive dialogues in which the analysand talks out loud to the self in disparaging and denigrating ways. The analyst finds herself eavesdropping on a dialogue between a speaking self and a self who is spoken to. The speaker seems to have little time for the listener within and he repeatedly castigates the spoken-to self.

On the surface, this might be understood simply as a classic pattern of anger turned inwards, of a grief preserved as a defiance. However, as the analyst listens and listens to this dialogue, every so often she will hear that the spoken-to self momentarily speaks back, usually in very brief references to the certitudes of the manic phase, to the truths of that golden era. These defiant moments of speaking are easy to miss: they will be cloaked immediately in a counter-narrative that preserves the mournful sense of apparently overwhelming loss. But when the spoken-to self speaks up in this way, I believe the manic depressive is revealing the existence of the ghost and the preservation of a secret relationship to the manic state.

I want to try to clarify this clinical observation. In both the manic and in the depressive states the person is split in two. The split of the ego involves a mothering figure and a nurtured infant, combined into one being. This combination represents a powerful, incestuous intercourse that destroys the father, thereby annihilating socialisation and the rules

of culture. It is this delusion of twoness in one, of the mother–child relation as a singular form of being, that is at the core of manic depressive
psychosis.

This unconscious delusion is a defence against a profound disorien-
tation and loss. At a crucial point in his development, this person has
been unable to leave the maternal order and move successfully into the
paternal order. Like the narcissistic personality, who forms a narcissistic
law, the manic depressive cannot find a way to make use of the internal
father. The retreat into an incestuous intercourse that is essentially auto-
erotic is a forlorn attempt to compensate for living in the limbo that
exists between the maternal and the paternal.

Axioms that constitute the logic of the manic depressive personality

As with the narcissist and the borderline it is useful to put into the first
person the sequence of this disorder, which is actually a form of order.

1. The hours, days, and weeks of my childhood are shrouded in an
   invisible inertness.
2. I know this shroud to be my family, whom I love.
3. We all live according to the same tempo and there is solace in shared
   suffering.
4. On occasion, mother or father shocks us with some stunning inspiration. It is as if a god has sent us a gift. It might be an object, such as
   a puppy, or a rhetorical moment, such as when father was promoted
   at work and took us out to dinner.
5. The stunning transformational moments remain etched in my mind.
   They are not memories so much as gathering points for unknown
   parts of myself.
6. School comes and I am unable to find my way. Other kids seem to
   know how to play together, how to enjoy life. I just yearn to be back
   home, in the known world of the family. This shields me from something but I do not know what that is.
7. Sometimes other kids find me amusing. Their acceptance brings me
   closer to them, and to things I have to offer about which I know very
   little. I experience the stirrings of joy.

8. I start to find my own thoughts rather exciting. They seem to arrive straight out of my mind.

9. My mind feels rather separate from me. I am inert, in hibernation, with no conscious ideas imbued with light.

10. Now and then my mind sends me an amazing daydream, an outstanding idea. It seems to be standing outside of me, waving to me to come and join in. I share some of these things with my new group of friends.

11. Mum and Dad have no idea what to do with these inspirations. Sometimes they are sad and withdrawn; sometimes they get cross and tell me to be quiet. My day-to-day self accepts these reproaches because in those precise moments I share their view. I too am shocked; I feel depressed and inert.

12. As I become adolescent and discover music, and books, and films, my mind finds its others. A partnership is born between my mind and the minds that have created these things. Streams of thought from authors, composers, historical figures, all connect with one another in vivid detail. My day-to-day self is shaken by these signs of hope. Will these saving visions free me from inertness?

13. I am unsure. These inspirations can suddenly fall away leaving me heavy and miserable. I don't know how to get on with the other kids. The mind that strikes me with amazing thoughts is not really me. My mundane self is always there, in waiting, like Mum and Dad at home.

14. As time passes I seem to find some golden road. The connecting threads seem more solid and reliable. If I let my mind go ... just let it rip ... if I let myself talk, or write, I seem to pave that road with hope. It helps me out of the slough of despond. I belong with the great minds; I am on a different path. I don't have to go home.

15. Then suddenly the lights go out. It was all just a dream. I see others forming love lives, careers, accomplishing their goals. They can connect their dreams to sustained reality, but I live on borrowed time. My visions that seemed to be such a gift are now turning people away from me.

16. My hope returns when God visits. Then I return to the human fold as the Second Coming. My mind is proof of this because it saves me each time, proving that I am the Messiah.

17. Mum and Dad have now passed, but they loved me. They sacrificed themselves and I gave up my child life for this. It is beginning to make sense.

18. But when I am dropped by the hands of God, I am back amongst the walking dead. I need Mum and Dad to return, to look after me. I feel an indescribable sadness. My mind has left me once again.

The psychoanalysis of manic depression

Perhaps because of the intensity of these remarkable and sometimes terrifying riffs of the mind, the manic depressive can seem untreatable. However, the analyst who is committed to seeing it through with this person, over many years of intensive work, enduring frightening highs and desperate lows, will experience the many sides of the picture in real time. This enables the two sides of the self to be brought into increasingly continuous contact with one another.

Alongside the work of analysis, these people survive because parents, spouses, children, and close friends stand by them. Perhaps without knowing, their quiet support and peristence help knit together the manic and depressive sides of this self, often a lifetime's work that goes uncelebrated.

I still hear from many patients whom I saw from the 1970s onwards, and I have found that particularly those who were manic depressive tend to keep in touch with me. We have a shared memory of our work together as being something of a risk. When we started out, we did not know whether five times a week on the couch would benefit them. As the decades have passed, it is clear that both of us were impressed by the power of the manic-depressive solution to early childhood issues, and by the intriguing ambivalence towards "recovery". Most of these analysands are now largely symptom free, with no further major manic episodes or prolonged depressions.

The heir to these oscillations is an informed mind which, as it looks back on the former episodes, seems to have achieved a third position. The more time passes, the more the mind has been liberated by memories of the self. Over time this person has become rather ordinary, and this can be a bit of a problem. The manic depressive self is extraordinary. Anyone who has been closely associated with someone who swings back and forth between mania and depression will know that their etchings last forever in the mind. The absence of these reminders becomes itself a form of presence. Ordinary sanity is distinctive, but also disappointing.

But you can't have everything.

Discussion

with Sacha Bollas, PsyD

The Narcissist

Q: *It seems that the narcissist is not truly nourished by the other as an individual but only by the other's participation in his own self system. Is he aware of this?*

A: Yes. Even his best relationships are based on strategies to gain advantage of one kind or another, so his self calculations nullify his ability to fold into the realms of intimacy. I think he is aware of this, and the pathos of the narcissist is deeply moving.

Q: *How should the analyst approach this aspect?*

A: It is useful for the analyst to acknowldge what a unique experience it is for this patient to be talking to an other in this way. Compared with how the narcissist speaks to himself, she will be addressing issues in a more transformative way. For example, if he is describing what he feels are ruthless strategies to promote himself, she might say something like: "And yet it is you—a part of you—telling me this about yourself." It is important to show him that when he is identifying what he regards as negative features of himself, there is another part of him that is, paradoxically, objectifying these dimensions as disturbing. The patient needs to be given credit for this.

Q: *How does the narcissistic dimension manifest in the transference?*

A: This is of course a very complex question. One aspect that I find very important is to note that however aggressively and angrily the narcissist may respond to what is said, he will return and help the analyst recover. She can therefore point this out in the transference in terms of the ways in which he unconsciously helps her in the work. In this way she is letting him know that he is showing a capacity for love and concern for the other.

Q: *So is the analyst simply trying to make the gang leader feel better about his empire building, or is there more to this?*

A: At a certain point in the work it will be important to explore the fact that the narcissistic laws and rulings are operating from only one part of the self's representational world. I often use the parliamentary metaphor to describe the divided views present in the mind. We live with many different ideas that derive from a wide variety of sources. All of us are accustomed to this sort of hurly burly. So the analyst can convey that she has understood the patient's dominant perspective, while at the same time making it possible to go on from there to seek others. For this to work, it is crucial that the person understands that the analyst has completely understood his position.

For example, let's say the patient is insisting that his problems have been caused by migrants who are destroying his life—taking over jobs, skiving off the state, etc. The analyst first needs to verbally mirror the analysand's lament. It may be as simple as, "It is clear that you believe that your lack of success is due to people coming here from abroad and depriving you of work." If she gives an accurate reflection of his comments, this becomes an interesting moment because it allows the patient to start to disagree with himself. He may add something: "Well, I understand that they need to find work …" By first mirroring his point of view, she has freed him to begin to connect with other views in his mind and to speak from a different position.

We may think of it as the irony of the echo. When we repeat the patient's toxic discourse so they hear it repeated by the other, then it changes its status. It has emerged from within the rage or distress of the self but when it is voiced by the other it shifts location, both literally and psychically. In this simple act of mirroring, the narcissistic patient will almost always modify or alter his assertions. If we view the initial definitive statement as the manifest content, it means that we then gain access to the latent meanings, not in this case by asking for free associations but by simply repeating what is said so that after-effects will emerge from the patient's psyche.

Q: *What motivates these after-effects?*

A: It is the implicit structure of the situation. When the analysand speaks, two people are listening. As he hears back what he has said, the patient becomes the one who can change the manifest content. This almost inevitably happens, as it occurs to him that what has been proposed is too extreme, or that he can see other sides to the issue.

Q: *So you wait for the patient to correct himself?*

A: Absolutely. This is the right of free speech in analysis. It is imperative that the analysand be free to speak whatever is on his mind, however odious it might be. It is important to support his narcissistic foundation. But then we wait. The patient may have said something with utter authoritarian finality, because the ambition of the ego is simply to get rid of the content at all costs. In Bion's sense, this is a –K evacuation. But once it is mirrored back and is heard as coming from outside the patient, then the eliminated becomes a potential object that can be thought about as if it originated from elsewhere.

So the patient has fulfilled the analytical dictat to speak what is in his mind, and he has done so by evacuating it into the toilet-breast of the analyst's mind (as Meltzer would have put it). There will then be an after-effect. When the analyst repeats the verbal structure of the elimination, and as the patient thinks about what was uttered-eliminated, his own thought process will begin to qualify the comment.

Q: *But what if he simply reiterates the validity of what he has said?*

A: Although he may try to justify the initial beta communication, and he may continue to propose it within the freedom of rhetorical choice, he will also offer qualifications of one kind or another. As time passes, as other qualifiers start to enter the picture, then the missile-state of the first verbal utterance gives way to a more dispersed meaning field and beta can no longer hold.

Q: *Alpha wins?*

A: Of course, because any time we subject an authoritarian point of view to further exploration it will break down. In time, the fecundity of the thought process itself challenges conscious certainties. The narcissist is wrapped up in well-tried rhetorical tropes. He has probably uttered the same lines, in one form or another, for much of his adult life. His listeners tend to tune out as these verbal missives are not intended as communication but only as a form of self positioning. Narcissists tend to be rhetorical territorialists, staking out claims based upon privileged knowledge or long-held conviction. So the last thing they are expecting is an attentive listener who seeks further associations.

Q: *So over time free association breaks down narcissistic rhetorical hegemony?*

A: Yes.

The Borderline

Q: *You say the borderline occupies the object by taking the object's pain into the self. Is this a form of introjection?*

A: Yes. The aim of inducing a perpetual state of pain is to sustain the maternal object that evoked it to begin with. So the experience of pain is the shadow of those experiences in infancy that occur in the name of the mother.

Q: *So in reality the mother may have been, in Winnicott's sense, a "good enough" mother?*

A: The actual mother may have little to do with the internal structure that is established in the baby. The labile and fluid nature of early infancy is too complex to be identified with a single external parental figure. However, a borderline mother will very likely communicate her idiom to the infant, who may then either take it into the self as a paradigm or utterly oppose it.

Q: *How would an infant oppose it?*

A: Obsessive-compulsive activities are a good way to oppose becoming the object of maternal pain. By turning it into one object of thought, then another and another, the self ingeniously creates options. The obsessive act is to displace actual life with mental possibilities. Doing this is a good way to turn an existential crisis into a mental one that may be controllled.

Q: *With the borderline patient, if dreaming and reality blend into one another with little difference, what are the clinical implications of this?*

A: Sessions are *in situ* dreams. The patient will usually begin by recounting an upsetting episode from his life, but this soon becomes saturated with affect. At this point he is finding "mother" in the matrix, and as the session continues this takes him deeper into the maternal order, unconsciously asking the analyst to be with him as he descends into the dense experience of dreaming. This is crucial, because to enable him to dream this internal reality the object must be constant. The double bind, however, is that for the borderline if it is to be constant it must be bad. Misery produces "mother". And this mother is guaranteed always to be there. The aim of a session is to set up this object as the primary one.

Q: *When you refer to the "borderline mix" are you suggesting that seeking the mix is pleasurable? As with Ben and Penny, who seem to enjoy taking turns in making one another miserable?*

A: It is true that for borderline partnerships this is a form of attachment. Both participants know they can rely upon the other to break bread every day over their miseries. In more successful borderline relations, the couple will find some malignant third object to elicit their fury and to provide them with an object of attachment to which they may return every day. Even though this seems a highly unstable form of relationship, it is often very ordered.

Q: *You write that the borderline is split by the mother (in the maternal order). This is an unusual departure from the psychoanalytic theory of splitting, which usually refers to the subject's splitting of self and object, not the subject as the object split by the parental other. How does this change your clinical work with such a person?*

A: I think it is axiomatic that this person has suffered repeated splits from the other. Frantz Fanon, when describing what it was to be objectified by white racism, stated that he was "overdetermined from without". This is true of the borderline who has been split by a kaleidoscopic other who mirrors her own mental confusion in her infant, so it is the child who becomes the bizarre object. When a child is split like this, being split becomes a part of his internal structure. The self becomes an odd container of happenstance assignments; he does not "add up". To use Winnicott's term, there is no "continuity of being", just a series of discontinuous attributions. With each projective characterisation by the maternal order, the infant's unconscious assimilates this and takes on the projections. Of course he does not consciously remember the experience, but the effect of being split by the other is that in subsequent relationships he is expecting a split and so he will invite it.

Q: *So borderlines will actually seek self–other relations in which they will be split?*

A: Unconsciously, yes. They seek intimacy, but they do this by joining the other in a festival of the negative. When they can get the other to attribute negativity to them, then they are in their familiar "discomfort zone".

Q: *You refer to "abstract forces" as a sort of object of desire.*

A: Borderlines have suffered eviscerative projective identification. They have been "gutted", so to speak. The particular has lost its identity and in its place is the trace of the annihilation of the particular, along with residual affect. They often cannot recall the details of an encounter but they can conjure the feelings that were evoked. So in working with the borderline the analyst might begin with abstract statements that reflect this undigested affect, then move from these explosive reactions to the originating event. Once this can be explored and understood, things begin to seem more rational. It is a therapeutic transformation from shattered affectivity to islands of sense. When this happens repeatedly over a long enough period, eventually the two of you begin to contact the patient's core self.

This core self never completely disappears—it is there in all of us—but the borderline core self was not mirrored and not elaborated in the maternal order. It was split by maternal anguish, it was designated as the receptacle of that anguish, so the devotion of the borderline is never to forget this form of love.

Q: *Love?*

A: Yes. Michael Balint referred to the "interpenetrating harmonious mix-up" of self and other. I would change it to the "interpenetrating disharmonious mix-up".

Q: *You refer to borderline allegorisation. Is this a form of transference?*

A: Yes. The act of allegory transfers a hazardous truth to a safer context. It also transfers the inchoate distress of a subject to a seemingly solid structure: a non-psychotic delusion. For the borderline, it works to move distressing internal phenomena to another realm entirely, which is the historic function of allegory.

Q: *How do you deal with this clinically?*

A: You translate. And this must be done many, many times. We are dealing here with the entrenched power of unconscious axioms established in the first years of life, so it will take time for the person to begin to understand you, to overcome the powerful habit of allegorisation. It means that they have to leave their "country of origin" to live in a new world, and this can produce a form of mourning.

The Manic Depressive

Q: *Turning to the manic depressive, your argument seems to be, in part, that this person suffers a sort of environmental deficiency. Does the lack of appropriate stimulation in childhood mean that this person is more likely to find internal events more nourishing?*

A: I do think that for the manic depressive internal mental events have usually been more vivid than parental engagement. In the somewhat dreary, depressed atmosphere of home, recollecting a dream from the night before, or engaging in daydreams, allows the child to turn to his own mind as stimulant. Of course, we all do this to some extent, but the absence of stimulation in the environment and in family relationships means that he gives particular weight to the singularity and priority of mental events.

Q: *Is this in part why these patients might tend to blank the analyst at first, because they do not have experience of meaningful intersubjective exchanges?*

A: Yes, that's a good way to put it. They are not accustomed to listening to others or to taking part in the mutual to-and-fro of conversation. Instead they want to spread the gospel that is arriving out of their minds, and this becomes an urge to convert others to their own way of seeing the world. Those who are deaf to their ideas then become the object of their contempt. Not being heard will have been a part of their history, but by adolescence the feeling of not being heard is a projective identification of the part of the self that listens to no one.

Q: *So when the analyst tries to get a point across, this is not just a matter of putting forward an interpretation.*

A: That is correct. It involves the gradual establishment of the intersubjective. For the manic depressive it is crucial that there is an other in the room who has a different mind, a different way of thinking, speaking, and communicating. The aim is first of all to develop this intersubjective matrix. With verbose manic patients, I learned that if I asked their permission to speak—"Do you mind if I tell you what I think?"—they would allow this. They were not accustomed to it, but luckily their sense of themselves as a perfect self meant that a simple request by the other must be granted.

Q: *So you gradually increase the opportunity to develop a dialogue with them?*

A: Yes. It can take years and one must be very patient. However, if you have a means of interrupting their grandiose rants, the mere act of interruption creates a potential space and you can get to a place of some dialogue. It is a way of indicating that someone else is in the room asking to be heard. It then becomes possible to start to comment on what they have said, and to invite them to reflect upon their own sermon.

Prior to this they have simply been delivering the word of God without reflecting on it at all. So the process of them hearing their own words changes the relationship. In Bion's terms, their speech is beta, but when the analyst repeats the very same wording, he transforms it to alpha. So the speech orginally uttered by the patient becomes a potential mental object of some use. Previously, talking was oral evacuation. No thought had been given to the evacuated. But as they start to tolerate and engage with this, you see them beginning to think the thoughts that arrived out of their own mind. So by mirroring their wording and getting them to think about what they have said, one introduces a different function of speech.

Q: *Does this slow the manic person down, and is this part of the reason you do this?*

A: Yes. The two-person relation slows down the one-person rant. The grandiose and compensatory appropriation of the function of the other is gradually lessened as the analyst is given the right of being an other with separate ways of thinking. Now for the person in a manic state, this slowing down will inherently be somewhat depressing. And so over time something like an ordinary depression begins to arrive to modify the manic state.

Q: *So the analyst actually introduces the depressive?*

A: It is the change in relational idiom that introduces it. The patient will gradually hear you receiving him and accurately echoing his statements. This evokes further associations, and these come from a part of him which is different from the pronouncing self. His own free associations break up the illusion of grandiosity, as he is progressively unsettled by wording and meaning that he assumed, of course, that he had fully understood.

Q: *So, as it did with the narcissist, free association helps to transform the psychic structures of this encounter?*

A: Yes, because, as it does with all of us, the complex thought process of unconscious thinking usurps the power of consciousness. As the manic depressive seeks to own that power, he discovers, sometimes to his dismay, that his conscious understanding of himself is limited and his unconscious knowledge is much greater than he realised.

Q: *But doesn't that lead them to become even more sure that their own minds contain ultimate power?*

A: That might appear to be a danger, but in fact when the analyst points out the logic of their free associations, and what this teaches both participants about the patient, they start to become genuinely puzzled by the thought process of their unconscious. The omnipotence of their conscious beliefs lessens, they are less sure of what they know about themselves, and in time they start to recognise the limits of consciousness. This produces a natural diminishment of the power of the spoken word.

The Three Characters

Q: *With all three characters discussed here, you seem to place consistent emphasis on specific mental structures that have been developed within them.*

A: I see all forms of psychopathology as intelligent decisions made by the ego under particular circumstances. They may be attempts to solve problems posed in the formative years, or they may be canny decisions made at any point in the life span at which, for innumerable possible reasons, something happens that the ordinary mind cannot cope with. One of the tasks of the analyst is to help these patients understand what they were up against, and that what is seen by themselves and others as a disturbance also represents an intelligent decision. So it is important to help them construct a history that makes the disorder explicable.

Q: *With all three characters it seems that a crucial technical component in the way you work is to offer the patient a lucid explanation for why they have become a distressed self. It also seems, however, that your style as an analyst, which is to encourage exploration of their free associations, is efficacious in itself.*

A: Yes. While I do think it is important at a certain point to gather the person's psychic history into a lucid explanation of why they have gone down the road they have chosen, it is equally important for the analyst to establish himself as other. Over time, as the patient free associates and the analyst responds, he gradually accepts the analyst as a listening other. This process creates a new mental structure. It will gradually alter the patient's character-pattern as it mitigates the more extreme forms of grandiosity and omnipotence of thought.

Q: *It seems that you place considerable weight on the idea of structuralisation. What do you mean by this, exactly?*

A: We can think of our DNA as providing the nuclei of structures to come. Consider the mother as someone who through her actions (which of course include her emotional states, the tones of her voice, her facial expressions, and so on) creates patterns that structure the infant's experience. The baby will internalise those structures that evolve in a dialectic between the mother's idiom and his own. By age two or three the toddler will have hundreds or thousands of inner patterns that are set in place. They have not been thought; they have been established through inter-action. They will generate innumerable axioms—theories of being and relating—specific to that self, derived and developed over time from the encounters between the self's internal world and the lived.

Q: *So when this person goes into analysis these axioms manifest themselves and the analyst encounters them?*

A: This is true, but it is important to understand that unconscious axioms are "presented", not represented. In my writing I make a basic differentiation between the presentational order and the representational order. The representational order is generally a form of prose: the person is telling you a consciously driven story about himself and its significance will be found in the content, the details of the story. The presentational order runs in parallel to this and it is a quite different form of communication. It is more poetry than prose. It concerns, not the *content* of what is said but what is communciated unconsciously through the *form* of the speaking. Whatever we might be intending to convey to the listener, our mental axioms or character axioms, our idiom of mind and behaviour, present themselves directly to the other and convey their own unconscious message. When some aspect of the person is communicated in the presentational order, we are in the realm of communication as action.

Q: *So in work with these three characters, a large part of the task is the negotiation of axioms essential to thoughtful communication between self and other?*

A: It is about communication between self and other, but it is also about the self's capacity to think about its own mental life. The cure, so to speak, is to help this person listen to himself in the session, to learn from his own unconscious, and to help him develop new and more generative conversations within himself.